Magic Islands

The San Juans
of
Northwest Washington

Magic Islands

A Treasure-Trove

of

San Juan Islands

Lore

By David Richardson

"There is no lover like an island shore
For lingering embrace;
No tryst so faithful as the turning tide
At its accustomed place."
Elizabeth Cutter Morrow

Copyright © 1964, 1965, 1970, 1995 by David Richardson

Printed and bound in the United States of America

Cover illustration by Bill Holm

ISBN 0-945742-08-8

Orcas Publishing Co.
Post Office Box 104
Eastsound, Washington 98245

Ferryboats ply the waters of the magic San Juans

Chapter One

The Magic Islands

High up in the northwest corner of Washington State lies a delightful archipelago of multi-sized, nature-blessed islands. Sea-girt, sky washed, and crowned with evergreens, the peaceful San Juans are an insular paradise whose special charms are without peer anywhere on the globe.

Archaeologically and spiritually, the San Juan Islands are a world apart. Archaeologically because the Islands actually are the last remaining mountain tops of a submerged continent, far older than the mainland of North America, now slowly receding, Atlantis-like, to a reluctant oblivion. Spiritually because–well, that takes some telling.

The San Juans have always seemed to have a special way of capturing your heart, turning your soul inside out, and handing you a whole new suit of values. Wealth doesn't always mean that much here, nor fame, not position. That fellow in the old clothes, driving a flivver, might be a millionaire living, for once, the way he really wants to. And the richest people in the Islands are sometimes the ones without a dollar in the bank.

Not that Island people are indolent. Most of them work as hard–or harder–than their mainland cousins. But the pressure is missing–pressure to meet a deadline, to "succeed" (whatever that means), to conform. There is no keeping up with the Joneses (after all, the Joneses aren't trying to keep up with *you)* and there is always plenty of time to be neighborly.

Newcomers–even weekend visitors–feel it, too. Often all it takes is to sense the throb of ferry engines, as you pull away from the dock at Anacortes, to start your nerves unwinding. By the time you've crossed Rosario Strait to Thatcher Pass, and you get your first close look at tree-lined, rock-bound shores rising steeply from peaceful blue waters, your tensions are gone and your blood pressure is down where it ought to be. Already you feel ten years younger! The Island Magic is indeed potent stuff.

Existence has never been as much of a struggle here as

7

elsewhere. It has been said of the Pacific Northwest that "no one need starve, if he can wait till the tide goes out," but in the San Juans you don't even have to wait for the tide. Fish still abound in both fresh and salt water, though not so much as formerly, there is still game to be found, and the woods are full of berries and other edibles. The soil is good enough that almost anyone can grow vegetables with a minimum of effort.

The weather is kinder, too. Summers in the Islands are cooler and winters are warmer than on the mainland. There is less rainfall, more sunshine; snow is infrequent. Pilots know even when the rest of the Pacific Northwest is socked in with fog or low clouds, the "banana belt" around the Islands is likely to be clear.

Occasionally the mild weather pattern is interrupted when the prevailing southwest wind shifts around to the northeast and, blowing across the frigid tops of the Canadian mountains, howls down upon the Islands, bringing ice and snow for a few days. But only for a few days, and then the temperature rises again, the snow melts, and life goes on as before.

Yet except for the severest northeasters–they only occur once every couple of years on average–the temperature rarely drops much below thirty degrees. The average winter temperature is well above freezing–some winters the average is in the forties–while in summertime the thermometer hovers around the seventy mark and hardly ever goes above eighty.

Long before the first white man set foot on the Islands their charms were known to the Lummi Indians, a peace-loving, easygoing tribe who found the living too easy here to be concerned with warring forays like their more bellicose neighbors to the north, south, and east.* According to Lummi tradition, the tribe is descended from a First Man, who dropped from the sky centuries ago to found their race. This aboriginal Adam lived on the northeast shore of San Juan Island, which is probably the nearest thing to the Biblical Garden of Eden he could have found in this part of the world.

Later the Lummi settlements were moved to Orcas Island and

*There is a connection between the name "Lummi" and the Chinook Jargon word *lamieh,* "old woman." The unwarlike Lummis were subject to some derision by the more aggressive tribes.

then, about a century ago, to the mainland. Today the Lummis live on Gooseberry Point, near Bellingham, just across Rosario Strait from their ancestral home.

The Indian influence is still felt in the San Juans, though not nearly so much as in former days. A few words of Chinook Jargon, the old trading language of the Northwest, still persist in daily conversation. "I'm not feeling too *skookum* today," one sometimes hears, *skookum* meaning strong or well. *Chuck* is often used for water; *tillikum* means friend; and very occasionally the old Indian greeting *klahowya* is heard. Other words live on in the names of ferries and other vessels. *Kaleetan* is an arrow; *Hiyu* (the smallest State ferry, oddly enough) means lots of, many; *Hyak* is fast; *Illahee* means land, or country; and so on.

How many islands are there? That depends on how you choose to count them. At low tide there are 768 islands, reefs, and rocks visible; at high tide the number drops to 457. If you count just the islands important enough to have names, you will come up with anywhere from 152 to about 180, depending on whose map you use, and whether you count double islands with single names once or twice, and so on. The two figures most often seen are 172 and 175, but even these numbers are more conventional than statistical.

The largest islands are San Juan, Orcas, and Lopez, which together comprise three quarters of the total land area. Other islands with an appreciable population are Waldron, Shaw, Stuart, Blakely, Decatur, Cypress, and Sinclair. In addition there are a number of one-family islands where the urge to get away from it all has been brought into full reality by the inhabitants.

Guemes, Fidalgo, and Whidbey Islands are geographically related to the San Juans and sometimes thought of as part of them. Again, whether the San Juans include these islands or just those in San Juan County, depends on who you talk to.

To the northwest another archipelago separates the San Juans from huge Vancouver Island. These are the Gulf Islands, under the Canadian flag, similar to the San Juans in physical appearance as well as in their charm and easygoing, insular way of life. The largest of these are Saltspring, Galiano, North and South Pender, Saturna, Mayne, Valdes, and Gabriola. Active Pass, which separates Mayne and Galiano, is a principal waterway used by boat traffic between Vancouver and Victoria, B.C., and is as busy as it is narrow.

Transportation is an important item everywhere in the San Juans. In pioneer days almost every family had its own sloop or, at least, rowboat. Now Washington State Ferries–one of the world's most extensive ferry systems–provide the "floating bridges" that connect the Islands to the mainland by means of frequent and regular schedules. Several small air services offer scheduled and charter flights between the islands and mainland towns as well, and a surprising number of local people fly their own planes–some out of their own airfields.

Indeed the nation's very first commuter airline began right here in the San Juans, just after World War II. For years Island Sky Ferries' small planes were our lifeline. They operated in the bush-pilot tradition, regularly landing on beaches and cow pastures where proper airfields had not yet been built. On islands without phones or radio, a bedsheet strung between two poles alerted passing pilots to the need for assistance–usually a medical emergency. Then there would be a return trip with the Islands' beloved country doctor, Malcolm Heath on board. Dr. Heath was justly famed for the manner in which he made his rounds by car, boat and plane to see patients scattered over the archipelago.

Those were days when planes rarely flew after dark. If you heard one in the night, everybody asked, "Who's sick?" Now in medical emergencies, day or night, evacuation to mainland hospitals is by helicopter and takes only minutes. All in all the San Juans are less isolated than they were, and more than a few islanders today commute to mainland jobs.

In former days much "commuting" was done by boat between the San Juans and the Canadian side of the border, and not all of it was legal. Smuggling of commodities ranging from opium and aliens to Prohibition hooch was widespread, due to the Islands' unique position astride the border, and to the many small, hidden bays where an illegal boatsman could put in to elude the customs men.

Many otherwise respectable citizens augmented their incomes by bringing in wool illegally. San Juan sheep farmers could buy the product cheaply in Canada, mix it with their own, and sell it at the higher American price. Knowing the number of sheep in the San Juans and the amount of wool shipped from the county, the government once calculated San Juan sheep had to be producing about 50 pounds of wool apiece!

Many legends surround men like Jim "Red" Kelly, also known as "Pig Iron" Kelly, and Larry "Smuggler" Kelly–no relation to each other–who were reputedly among the most resourceful and daring of the San Juan smugglers. Certain operators of the period would reportedly bring in alien Chinese for $50 or more a head and, if pursued, call up their passengers one at a time, hit them over the head, and shove them over the side to destroy the "evidence."

Old-timers who knew them deny that San Juan smugglers were really that bloodthirsty.

A boatload of Chinese was once unloaded on a rock between San Juan and Lopez at night, and the passengers told they were on the mainland, and that a large town was situated "just over the hill." Next morning the Chinese went over the hill to discover nothing there but more water. They were found a week later, hungry but alive, by a passing preacher. The island is still known as China Rock.

The Revenue Service was given a merry chase by these adventurers in early years. The Service's fastest launch, *Scout,* was finally laid up because it was too slow to catch anything with its top speed of four knots. In 1895 it was remodeled and given a 40-horse engine with a speed of 12 knots, but still the smugglers' boats could outmaneuver the *Scout* when they couldn't outrun her. The *Scout*'s usual companion was a sleek cutter, universally if irreverently called the "Black Pup." The "Pup's" glory was a shiny copper smokestack, but it was eclipsed by the ugliness of the canvas lean-to that formed her only cabin.

In Prohibition days the rum-runners stationed lookouts on high promontories to watch the activities of government boats and light signal fires when the coast was clear. Then high speed boats crossed on a bee-line from the B. C. side. Fast cars transported the goods to other boats which crossed to the mainland on the next "all clear" signal.

Indian canoes were sometimes used to carry liquid cargoes,

while another favorite trick was to sail a small boat right next to the ferry, on the side away from the American mainland, to get through unobserved.

Today it is the purveyors of hard drugs that pass through the San Juans on occasion–and are caught on occasion–but these traffickers are apparently few and their methods less colorful. The little smugglers' boats are gone from the scene. You'll no longer see them plying furtively among the islands of the "rock pile," as ferry skippers call the reef-studded Yellow Island area. In more recent years, though, you might have seen something else there to make you blink. For in the middle of the "rock pile" is little Coon Island, long-time home of Jack Tusler, a man with a rare sense of humor.

Just opposite Coon a small rock, only a few feet in area and hardly a speck on the chart, barely shows above the surface. It lies in the middle of the channel the smaller ferries used to follow on some trips to Sidney, B.C. Tusler used this rock as a stage for performances that left ferry passengers gawking. Once he had an island girl sit there in a mermaid costume, mirror in hand, combing her long hair like a legendary Rhine River siren. Another time he mimed a white-coated "surgeon" extracting a string of sausages from a patient's innards. He would have Indians smoking peace pipes, or a barber cutting somebody's hair, or set up a bridge party complete with a table and four players–all oblivious, of course, to the dumbfounded stares of the ferry riders. Skippers claimed they could actually feel the ferry list to one side when the "Commodore of Coon Island" staged one of his spectaculars, and all the passengers moved to the side of the boat to see it.

Tusler no longer holds sway on Coon, and today's ferry riders must content themselves with merely watching the spectacular scenery or, not infrequently, the antics of passing porpoises and killer whales. Still, ferry skippers may–and sometimes do–vary their routes to give passengers an extra scenic thrill.

Ordinarily these minor deviations do not lead to the sort of mishap produced by the ferry Elwha's 1983 detour into Grindstone Harbor, off Orcas Island's southeast shore.

The skipper figured he had just enough room to wheel his 382-foot-long vessel into and out of this narrow bay without grazing the reef that guards it, but he figured wrong. With a sickening crunch the ferry slammed full-bore onto the reef (henceforth immortalized as "Elwha Rock") and came to an abrupt stop there. Fortunately, the only significant injuries were to the ferry itself and to the immediate plans of her passengers–not to mention the hapless ferry captain's reputation.

Subsequent investigation revealed that the skipper was entertaining a passenger, a lady friend whose home fronts on Grindstone Harbor, and wanted her to see what her place looks like from the water.

The mishap led to (among other consequences) a local pop group's recording a song which gained considerable radio play for a time. It's called "Elwha on the Rocks" and the most memorable line goes:

"Hiya, Cutey! Wanna see my wheelhouse?"

Friday Harbor's attractive waterfront

Chapter Two

Juan de Fuca: the Man Who Wasn't There

Or was he? Historians say he wasn't, yet the Islands are probably named for him, at least indirectly, and legend says he discovered the broad inlet to Washington's inland sea exactly two hundred years before Captain George Vancouver explored it and found Puget Sound.

Juan de Fuca, whose real name was Apostolos Valerianos, was a Greek sea captain who sailed the Pacific in the late 1500's for the Spanish. He claimed to have discovered, on one of his trips along what we now know as the northwest coast of the United States, a "broad inlet of sea" in which he sailed for three weeks and found land and waterways trending in almost every direction of the compass.

This was in 1592–exactly one hundred years after Columbus' discovery of America–and it was not uncommon for down-and-out sailors to claim to have discovered all sorts of things. When de Fuca came to Italy and told of his "discovery" no one paid much attention, except an Englishman, John Lok, whose main interest in life just then was to find the fabled "Northwest Passage" from the Atlantic to the Pacific.

Lok was convinced de Fuca had discovered that very passage, and spent years trying to raise money for an expedition to prove it. De Fuca died, however, before an expedition could be launched.

De Fuca's story was eventually published in a book which had a large readership in the next two centuries, and belief in the existence of de Fuca's strait was widespread. Therefore, when the fur trader, Charles Barkley, discovered the entrance to a broad strait off the northwest coast, not far from where de Fuca reported it, Barkley supposed he had found Juan de Fuca's strait, and gave it that name.

Historians today believe de Fuca's story was a hoax, and that the actual existence of a strait so close to the position claimed by him is a pure coincidence.

The main reasons for disbelieving the old Greek sea captain's tale are, first, there is no record in any of the old-world archives of the voyage de Fuca claimed to make, and second, most of his description of the strait and its position is inaccurate.

Nevertheless de Fuca's story has some ring of truth and probably we will never know whether he was here or not. If he was, the "divers Ilands" he reported seeing inside were surely the San Juans, which would make him the first white man to see them.

Barkley discovered (or rediscovered) the strait in 1787, but didn't enter far enough to see the San Juans. The first to do so was Manuel Quimper, a Spanish explorer, who saw the Islands but mistook them for a part of the mainland to the north. Quimper discovered Haro Strait, which he named for his pilot, Gonzalo Lopez de Haro.

A year afterward another Spaniard, Francisco Eliza, took an expedition of two sailing vessels into the strait and sent the schooner *Santa Saturnina* into the Islands to give them a good looking over.

The *Santa Saturnina* was piloted by First Pilot Juan Pantoja y Arriaga. Beginning at the Spanish base at what is now Esquimalt, on the southern tip of Vancouver Island, the little party sailed northward along the British Columbia coast as far as the lower edge of Saltspring Island.

Pantoja called this island "Isla de Sayas" after a sailor friend of his, but Eliza overruled him afterward and the name which went down on the first chart was "San Eusebio."

Pantoja reconnoitred North and South Pender Islands in a small boat by moonlight, and the next day the *Santa Saturnina* nosed into Plumper Sound, which separates the Penders from Saturna. Then, rounding Saturna's East Point, they discovered the broad reaches of Georgia Strait, to which Pantoja gave the name of "Rosario." Spanish for "Rosary," the name now applies to the narrower strait to the south which divides the San Juans from the U. S. mainland.

Pantoja then sailed eastward to a small island he named "Patos," meaning ducks; and Patos it is still called today.

In the next few days the party visited the Sucia group and Matia, and probably Barnes and Clark Islands. Somewhere in the area they sought refuge from a southeast storm which lasted two

15

days. The rest of the time the wind hardly blew at all, so that Pantoja had to put his men to rowing in order to make any headway.

Pantoja also gave Sucia (SOO-shuh) its present name. In Spanish it means "dirty" or, in sailor's talk, "rocky." Matia he called originally "Mal abrigo" or "Bad Anchorage," and that name was later shortened to its present form, pronounced MAY-shuh by locals. The explorers turned back after reaching the vicinity of Lummi Island, this time following the north coast of the San Juans where they saw a number of whales. These are called "orcas" in Spanish and that, residents like to believe, is how Orcas Island came to be named. Some historians, though, theorize that the name is in fact short for Horcasitas–and meant to honor Revilla Gigedo de Orcasitas, who was viceroy of Mexico at the time, and sponsor of Eliza's expedition.

Pantoja passed near Waldron, which he named "Lemos," and the group of islands including Stuart, Johns, and Spieden, which he called "Moraleja." Flattop Island, Parker's Reef, and Henry Island were seen and written onto the chart, but were not named. San Juan, seen from a distance, was believed to be part of Orcas.

Pantoja returned to Esquimalt and told Eliza in glowing terms about the beautiful but "indescribable" archipelago around which he had traveled, but warned that the area was full of rocks and too dangerous to navigate in any but the smallest vessels. Consequently the Spanish did not go into the archipelago's interior that year, although they did make another short reconnaissance along the southern part of the island group. On this trip Eliza's other pilot, Don José Narvaez, discovered Smith and Minor Islands, naming them "Islas de Bonilla," and paid a brief visit to the southern coast of Lopez, which Narvaez also took to be a part of San Juan and Orcas.

In 1792 the Spanish were back to do some more exploring in the area, but they were beaten to it by Captain Vancouver, who had passed by in the spring on his way to discovering Puget Sound.

Passing the San Juans, Vancouver was intrigued by this appealing group of big and little, high and low islands, and he sent one of his lieutenants, William Broughton, to look them over. Broughton's reconnaissance provided the first look at the interior of

16

the Islands.

Broughton took one of Vancouver's two vessels, the *Chatham,* across the strait from Port Discovery and entered the narrow, rocky passage between Lopez and San Juan on May 18, 1792. The *Chatham* sailed up Griffin Bay, rounded Turn Point, and anchored that night off the southern tip of Shaw Island.

Next morning Broughton sent a pair of small boats up San Juan Channel and sailed in the *Chatham* up Upright Channel. They only went a couple of miles when the Englishmen found the delightful low, sandy beach now known as Flat Point. They anchored there and spent the rest of the day fishing and, perhaps, loafing in the fine spring weather.

On the 20th Broughton continued through Upright Channel to a large bay at the entrance to East Sound. In small boats, the party explored both Lopez Sound to the southeast and Harney Channel to the northwest. Near Blind Bay they came upon a small Indian village and traded with the Indians for some fresh venison and one live fawn.

*The British exploring ships
Discovery and Chatham*
Vancouver City Archives

The following day was spent towing the *Chatham* through the tricky cross currents toward Obstruction Island and through one of the narrow passes into Rosario Strait.

Here the tide caught the *Chatham* and drifted her against the rocks on the coast of Orcas. The men worked quickly to get the vessel back into safe waters, but in so doing they lost their lead and sounding line.

Finally they reached a safe depth and anchored. Again the small boats were sent out to explore the islands to the east–Cypress, Lummi,

17

and Sinclair.

On the 22nd Broughton's little party crossed Rosario Strait and anchored in a charming bay on the west shore of Cypress, where the men found delicious wild strawberries in abundance. Although Broughton himself did not name any of the islands or features he found in the San Juans, he did call this "Strawberry Bay" in his report to Vancouver, and the Captain let this name stand on the chart, as it still does today.

The party left the San Juans the next day to sail south to rendezvous with Vancouver, who was anchored then just off the southern tip of Bainbridge Island, across from the present city of Seattle.

Later the *Chatham* and Vancouver's other ship, the *Discovery,* paid the islands another visit. Vancouver himself stopped on Minor Island and took a number of observations there to help determine the location of the various mountain peaks that were visible: Mt. Rainier, Mt. Baker, Mt. Saint Helens and Mt. Hood were observed and their positions added to the map.

On June 8, Vancouver sailed into Strawberry Bay on Cypress once again. Broughton, in the *Chatham,* attempted to do likewise but the tide drifted him into the rocks on the southern shore. The stream anchor was thrown out quickly but the line parted and the anchor was lost. The crew spent a day or more dragging the bottom in an attempt to recover the anchor, but were unable to do so. The anchor, presumably, is still there.

Vancouver remained on Cypress a couple of days. To prevent scurvy among his crew he put them to work brewing "spruce beer," and also had them collecting wild onions which grew there, as well as replenishing the ships' water supplies.

Vancouver called the island "Cypress" for the many tall evergreens he found there and mistook for cypress trees.

On the 10th the *Discovery* and *Chatham* left Cypress and sailed out the north end of Rosario Strait about the same time the Spanish were entering it at the south end in two ships of their own. These were the *Sutil* and *Mexicana* commanded by Dionisio Alcala-Galiano and Cayetano Valdés. They had just come from an anchorage on the southern shore of Lopez where they had corrected their chronometers by setting up a telescope to observe the transit of

18

one of the moons of Jupiter.

Vancouver and the Spanish explorers were unaware of each other's presence until finally they met in Boundary Bay, north of Bellingham. Both parties continued their explorations of the waterways to the north of the San Juans, where they circumnavigated Vancouver Island and returned to the Pacific by that route.

Most of the names that had been bestowed upon the San Juans were Spanish, as Vancouver's party did little formal naming, mostly recording descriptions like "Sandy Island" (Minor) or "Peaked Hills" (Watmough Head on Lopez).

This is all to the good, as most of the Spanish names are light and musical and quite in keeping with the Islands' mood.

In 1841 Captain John Wilkes, who was sent by Congress to survey the coasts of America, came to the San Juans and proceeded to change all the names to some that suited him better. The whole group he called "Navy Archipelago"; San Juan became "Rodgers Island," and Lemos he named "Waldron." The latter name stuck but, fortunately, the others didn't.

Wilkes also named Shaw Island, Jones, Clark, and Obstruction Islands, and he named some prominent features of the Islands, notably Mt. Constitution, President Channel, Point Lawrence, Peapod Rocks, Point Doughty, etc., names which are still in use.

Chapter Three

The Pig That Almost Started a War

*A*lthough all the northwest country was claimed, at one time, by four nations–England, Spain, Russia, and the United States–none of these countries seemed to care or even know much one way or the other about the San Juan Islands in particular. For half a century they remained the domain of roving Indian bands. Very occasionally, an intrepid French-Canadian trapper would pass by.

In 1844, the battle for the White House centered around the slogan of James Polk, "54-40 or fight," meaning Polk intended to insist on America's claim to the Northwest territories as far north as Alaska. Two years later we settled for a boundary along the 49th parallel between Canada and America, but because of inattention to the San Juans by both sides, the treaty was worded in an ambiguous way that could have put the Islands on either side of the line.

Meantime, in 1845, the powerful Hudson's Bay Company had "taken possession" of San Juan Island by landing on it and erecting a wooden tablet to that effect, on a hillside near Cattle Point.

In 1850 the H. B. C. established a small fishing station at Eagle Cove and learned the Indian method of reef-netting salmon, which they salted and shipped to company forts scattered around the territory.

Two years later the company's steamer *Beaver* landed 1300 sheep to graze on the island's pastures and established a post, named "Bellevue Farm," there. Charles Griffin was left in charge along with a small group of sheepherders brought from Hawaii.

The first little party of American settlers showed up in 1853 but was soon frightened away after a raid by northern Indians.

Meanwhile the Islands had been listed by the Oregon Territorial Legislature in 1852 as part of Island County, and in 1854 the U. S. Collector of Customs for Puget Sound, Isaac Ebey, showed up and tried to collect taxes from Bellevue Farm. Griffin declined to pay, claiming the island was not American, but British territory.

The next day an official party from Victoria arrived and tried to arrest Ebey who, whipping out a pistol, refused to be taken.

Ebey left the island without collecting any taxes and no further efforts were made until 1855 when the new Washington Territorial Legislature put the Islands in Whatcom County. It wasn't long before that county's go-getting sheriff, Elias Barnes, was knocking on Griffin's door with a tax bill for about $80.

When Griffin refused to pay, Barnes seized forty head of prized breeding rams and auctioned them off at fifty cents to a dollar apiece to eight "bidders" he just happened to have brought with him. Since the total collected was less than the tax, he sold a few sheep also, at one or two cents a head.

Barnes' party was about to load the stock into their small boats when Griffin and a band of the Kanaka shepherds, armed with knives, charged noisily down upon them. Barnes called to his companions "in the name of the United States" to defend their property, which they did at pistol point.

Griffin sent to Victoria for help but by the time the company's steamer *Beaver* arrived on the scene Barnes' party was safely back in Bellingham Bay.

Britain filed an official protest over Barnes' act, asking 3,000 pounds damages.

Since the heart of the dispute was the unsettled boundary, a commission representing both countries was set up to look for a solution. Of course neither side had any intention of agreeing to any settlement that did not give them the disputed territory.

While the diplomats muddled, American and British settlers began arriving on the island. One of the Americans was a disappointed Fraser River gold miner, Lyman A. Cutlar,* whose farm was near the H. B. C.'s post overlooking Griffin Bay. Cutlar had a small patch of garden in which he frequently discovered a pig, owned by Griffin, rooting up his potatoes.

Cutlar visited Griffin in a huff. "You'll have to keep that d--- pig out of my potatoes," he told Griffin, to which the Englishman is said to have replied, "I think you'd better keep your potatoes out

---

*Or Cutler as it is sometimes spelled. National Parks researchers, and others, currently lean toward "Cutlar."

of my pig!"

Not long afterward, when Cutlar found the erring porker trespassing yet again in his potato patch, he flew into a rage and, as he later recalled it, "upon the impulse of the moment I seazed my rifle and shot the hog."

When Cutlar told Griffin what he'd done he offered to pay for the pig, but Griffin refused to accept Cutlar's offer and, instead, swore out a warrant for his arrest. When a British officer landed to serve the paper, the "criminal" went into hiding to escape being taken to Victoria for trial.

As tension between British and Americans mounted on the island one Yankee settler, Charles McKay, rowed over to Whatcom (Bellingham) and purchased the largest American flag he could find. A few days later–July 4, 1859–the flag was flown from a pole in front of the home of Paul K. Hubbs, the new Deputy Collector of Customs, in celebration of Independence Day.

Three days later the flag was still flying when Brigadier General William L. Harney, the American military commander in the region, passed by (not totally by accident) on the steamer *Massachusetts*. Harney landed briefly to talk to the American settlers, who promptly complained to him about the British actions on the island.

Harney subsequently, using the pretext of protecting the settlers from Indians, sent a company of infantry under Captain George E.

George E. Pickett

Pickett to San Juan from Fort Bellingham. Pickett landed with his sixty men on July 27, just as a British magistrate was arriving from Victoria with orders to apprehend Cutlar.

Pickett posted a proclamation on the beach declaring the island to be United States territory, and not subject to any laws or courts except those of the United States.

The British answered by dispatching Lieutenant G. P. Hornby and a force of men from the navy base at Esquimalt to "drive the Americans from the island." Hornby arrived in Griffin Bay on *H. M. S. Tribune,* along with a force of Royal Marines on the *Plumper.* Hornby invited Pickett to meet him on board the *Tribune* for a chat, but Pickett declined and made the British officer come to his tent on the beach.

Hornby told Pickett his orders were to land and he hoped there would be no bloodshed in carrying those orders out. Pickett, however, assured him the Americans–though vastly outnumbered –would "fight until the last man" if the British tried to land their forces.

Hornby was convinced Pickett wasn't bluffing and so he did not land, but sent for reinforcements. Before long the British numbered 2,140 men and had five ships in the bay with 167 guns. Pickett wrote to his commanding officer that his little force would be "merely a mouthful" for the British.

About this time Rear Admiral R. L. Baynes, commander of the British Pacific Fleet, arrived on the scene and ordered the forces in Griffin Bay not to try to land, or to provoke any kind of conflict, saying he "would rather shed tears than blood" over a mere pig.

Word of the events had also reached Washington by now and President James Buchanan sent Lieutenant General Winfield Scott, commander in chief of the Army, to the island to try to set things right and preserve peace. Scott quickly proposed to Governor Douglas, in Victoria, a joint occupation of the island by one hundred men from each side, and dual sovereignty of the San Juans until the Islands' ownership had been determined by the two governments.

The proposal was accepted by the British and so on March 20, 1860, a force of 100 British landed on the north end of San Juan Island and established themselves on Garrison Bay, while the

American encampment on the south end was reduced to the same number.

By request of the British, contained in a secret message to Scott, Pickett was removed from command of the American Camp, or "Fort San Juan" as it became known. With the beginning of the Civil War, Pickett–being a Southerner–left the Northwest to join the Confederacy, and later gained fame as the leader of the brave but bloody Southern charge at Gettysburg. The two garrisons were maintained on San Juan throughout the war.

Finally in 1871 America and Great Britain agreed to submit the question of the San Juans' sovereignty to arbitration by the Emperor of Germany who decided, the following year, in favor of the United States. Accordingly, the English camp on Garrison Bay was vacated and only the American flag was left flying on the island.

The occupation saw the island's first town established near the old Hudson's Bay Co.'s Bellevue Farm, and the first road–still called "the military road"–which led down the center of the island from one camp to the other. Settlers had been arriving in increasing numbers, but because of the unsettled sovereignty they were not

English Camp on Garrison Bay, San Juan Island,
shortly after the British landing in 1859
Provincial Archives, Victoria, B.C.

able to stake formal land claims, but merely squatted wherever it suited them.

Since there was no clear sovereignty there were no taxes and no laws either, and the military commanders were hard put to keep the peace. Whiskey flowed freely and all sorts of misdeeds went unpunished, as the offenders would claim American citizenship if caught by the British, and British citizenship if apprehended by American authorities, thus avoiding the jurisdiction of both.

The military garrisons meanwhile were getting along beautifully and there was much neighborly wining and dining of one another.

After the settlement San Juan's residents were able at last to file for homesteads on their lands. English Camp itself was homesteaded in 1875 by William Crook, whose family lived for some time in one of the British barracks. Crook's son James and a daughter, Mary Davis, continued to live at English Camp after his death. They looked after the place, patiently acting as guides for occasional tourists who came around, and kept a few Pig War mementos in a sort of museum corner of their farm home. Crook also tended a small cemetery on the slopes of nearby Mount Young, where were buried several British soldiers who died during the occupation.

Crook received an annual check from the naval establishment at Esquimalt in appreciation for this latter service, but there were

American forces on San Juan Island, soon after the landing
National Park Service

*The old British blockhouse at English Camp on San
Juan Island, a perennial tourist attraction*
National Park Service

no funds to keep up the camp buildings, which largely deteriorated over the years.

Only in 1966 was a San Juan Island National Historical Park finally created, thus preserving some 1750 acres of the two former military sites and providing federal funds for their upkeep. Some structures have now been restored, notably English Camp's barracks, hospital and commissary buildings, and the much-photographed beach-front log blockhouse.

At American Camp the defensive earthworks built on bare, high ground are still plainly visible. Access roads, a parade ground fence and an interpretive center have been built, but there are few other structures. Most of this part of the Park is natural and open, with pleasant hiking trails, quiet beaches and picnic grounds.

Park researchers know pretty well from old pictures, documents and archaeological excavations just how the two garrisons were laid out and what sort of life it was for the soldiers and their families. Park employes and volunteers in period costumes act as guides and sometimes reenact scenes from those eventful days.

The locations of the Hudson's Bay Company farm and other places important to the Pig War saga are known and can be visited by history buffs. What has not yet been definitely determined is the precise spot where Lyman Cutlar angrily dispatched the lowly pig–the "war's" lone casualty.

Chapter Four

Pioneer Days in the San Juans

Charles Griffin, the manager of the Hudson's Bay Company's Bellevue Farm, is generally credited with being the Islands' first white resident. Very likely he was preceded, though, by a man named Verrier, a French-Canadian trapper who took up residence on Orcas Island. Descendants say this was as early as 1843. Verrier trapped beaver, mink, and coon and sold the skins to the H. B. C.

Other French-Canadians came along to form the nucleus of a community on Orcas, among them men with names like Iotte, LaPlante, and LaPorte, some of whose descendants still live in the Islands.

The first wave of American settlers arrived as gold was discovered on the Fraser River and the Islands became a stopover point for miners on their way north. When the rush slowed to barely a crawl in 1858 some of the disappointed gold-seekers found their way back to the San Juans and settled here. Among these were Charles Shattuck, who built his home near the present village of Eastsound, and William Moore, the first to settle at Olga. On San Juan the first permanent settlers were Dan W. Oakes and Charles McCoy–who changed his name to McKay when he arrived–both of them erstwhile Fraser River gold miners, as was Lyman Cutlar, who fired the one and only shot of the pig war.

With the establishment of American and British military posts on San Juan the Islands' settlement increased rapidly. One of the newcomers was Stephen Boyce, who came to the island planning to open a store. The military, though, had its own trading post and refused to let him open another one in competition, so Boyce traded his stock for some property near the fort, on which he and his family squatted until the boundary settlement opened the Islands for homesteading. Boyce went on to become a founding father of Friday Harbor, as well as the Islands' first sheriff, a founder of the first school, and so on.

The post sutler, or storekeeper, at Fort San Juan was Captain

Edward D. Warbass, a well known pioneer not only of the Islands but of all the Puget Sound country. He played an important part in the Indian War of 1855, was the first postmaster north of the Columbia River, the first representative of Whatcom County in the Territorial Legislature, and a deputy collector of customs at Roche Harbor for many years, besides serving in many other local and state offices during his long life.

McKay, Boyce, and several others organized the first church in the Islands, which is generally believed to be the second Presbyterian church established in Washington, if not the first. Money and labor were donated by settlers in 1860 or 1861. The little log building was used both for religious services and as a schoolhouse.

The first resident minister was the Reverend T. J. Weekes, a young missionary from England. Weekes stayed on the island for years and, most of that time, was the county's only resident preacher.

In 1865 a separate schoolhouse was built on what was known as Portland Fair Hill and a "sure-nuff school ma'rm" was hired for $30 a month to come to the island and teach. Her name was Margaret Naylor. She and the Reverend Weekes were later married.

Portland Fair Hill schoolhouse on San Juan Island

The origin of the name "Portland Fair Hill" is forgotten now. The site is down towards American Camp in the south central part of San Juan Island.

The present Valley Church at Madden's Corners was begun in 1878, completed in 1882, and lovingly restored to its original condition by volunteers in 1949. (Actually, this pretty pioneer church isn't in a valley at all, but was built on high ground overlooking the island's fertile central plain.)

On the other islands settlement occurred more slowly. In 1859, while the white population on San Juan was 30, there were only three or four people other than Indians living on Orcas, and probably not more than five or six on all the other islands put together.

An early store was established in the 1860s by Paul K. Hubbs at Grindstone Bay, near the village of Orcas. Old-timers say the bay got its name because Hubbs had the only grindstone on the island and settlers had to come there to sharpen their knives and other tools.

Like so many early settlers, Hubbs had an Indian wife. When she died he purchased from an Indian father another bride–a beautiful young girl for which he paid four sacks of flour, a musket, powder and shot, and two blankets. Hubbs was 70 at the time, and the girl ran away before the marriage could take place. It is not recorded whether the purchase price was refunded.

As late as 1883 white women were rare on Orcas. According to Peter Legbandt, who settled near Doe Bay, his German wife was the only white woman between Point Lawrence and East Sound.

An early settler on Lopez Island, H. E. Hutchenson, is said to have come to the Islands in the early fifties. Rounding the point of Fisherman's Bay one day he came upon a group of local Indians fighting off a party of Northerns. Hutchenson joined the battle and helped drive off the marauders, for which the local Indians rewarded him with a home and proclaimed him a hero. Hutchenson ran a store at Lopez Landing for many years.

Another name closely associated with Lopez is Arthur "Billy" Barlow, father of the legendary Captain Sam Barlow, who spent his lifetime in the San Juans piloting boats through the intricate waterways in and around the islands. The elder Barlow, an English

29

sailor, jumped ship in Esquimalt one night and crossed the strait in an Indian canoe to New Dungeness. Later, in 1856 he settled on Lopez' southwest shore at a place now known as Barlow Bay.

Most of the settlements in those days were on the water, and nearly every family had a boat of some kind in which to do their traveling. Those early islanders thought little of rowing half a day to a distant store for supplies. Lyman Cutlar's anger over the pig, rooting in his potatoes, is more understandable in view of the fact that Cutlar had rowed a boat all the way to the Olympic Peninsula and back for the seed potatoes he planted in his little patch.

Inland there were few roads good enough even to ride horseback. Communications were slow. There were no doctors. Why, then, did people come to the Islands at all? No doubt for the same reason as today: the aura of peace and contentment that seems to be the Islands' trademark was just as real then as it is now. Those early settlers must have felt the same all-rightness, the same relaxing of the nerve fibres, that we–whether residents, summer people, or visitors–still know today, just being here.

And yet there were grim times, too. On San Juan, lawlessness was barely kept under control during the occupation years. Gun-toting, land-grabbing, illicit whiskey trafficking and many other kinds of crime flourished in boisterous San Juan Town, much as in the rip-roaring frontier towns depicted for us on TV and movie westerns.

After the boundary settlement, things quieted down considerably, but San Juan has always somehow seemed a bit on the brash side compared with a more settled way of life on the other islands.

One real-life series of events on San Juan in the early 1870s rivals Hollywood's best plots for blood-curdling drama. When the soldiers were removed from the island the San Juans became a part of Whatcom County. Stephen Boyce was made sheriff. He had hardly assumed the office when he got his first case: a murder involving an Englishman, Samuel Fuller, whose body was found, half-covered with boulders, under a madrona tree. No clues to the murderer's identity were found, but as Fuller was a man of means, the motive seemed to be robbery.

The next year Harry Dwyer, a farmer, was found shot to death in a furrow of the field where he had been plowing. His team of

San Juan Island pioneers: Edward Warbass,
Charles McKay, and Stephen Boyce

horses was still standing in the traces, and had dug out great holes in trying to get free. But the reins were still around the victim's shoulders and Dwyer was a very large man. Nearby was Dwyer's house and inside lay his wife, Selina, who had also been shot to death. Scattered about the porch were some baby clothes she had been sewing, as they were expecting a baby that summer.

Dwyer had recently sold a boat for cash, and the money was presumed to have been stolen by the murderer.

A neighbor girl, Lila Hanna, recalled loaning her brother's gun to a half-Kanaka, half-Indian youth, Joseph Nuanna, the day of the murder. The boy had acted strangely when he returned the gun, and a shot pouch belonging to it was missing. Lila's mother told Boyce about her suspicions, and Boyce went to arrest Nuanna. He found that Joe and a companion named Charlie had fled in a canoe for Victoria.

Boyce pursued the fugitives to Victoria where he managed to have them apprehended. Charlie was released for lack of evidence but Joe, after extradition proceedings, was returned for trial. Nuanna stoutly maintained his innocence right up to the point in the trial where he was confronted with the shot pouch, which Boyce had found near the Dwyers' house.

Nuanna then confessed not only that he killed Fuller, as well as the Dwyers, but that these were merely the first in a whole series of

31

murders he planned. He even named all his intended future victims in the order he planned to do away with them.

Nuanna was condemned to hang at Port Townsend for his crimes, and suffered horribly when the noose malfunctioned and left him slowly strangling to death. His last words had been a grumbled complaint that the coffin provided by the county for his remains was unpainted.

Two of the names on Nuanna's list were John and Bill Keddy, bachelors living near the north end of the island on a hill still called Cady's mountain–the spelling somehow having changed over the years. The Keddys, unnerved by what they considered a very close call, sold out and left the island soon afterward.

The removal of the military establishments was the beginning of the end for San Juan Town–the notorious little village on Griffin Bay, once described as "bedlam day and night," where most of the stores were saloons and women were unsafe on the streets at any hour. After the army's trading post closed there, a civilian store was opened by Israel Katz, a merchant who divided his time between San Juan Island and Port Angeles. As the commercial and residential development of the island shifted northward, the store changed hands two or three times. The post office was moved to a place called Mac's Landing, later named "Argyle" after the Scotsman who had a mill there. San Juan gradually turned into a ghost town.

Then on a hot summer day in 1890 a caretaker known as "Whispering Pete" Seary (so-called because the old bull-teamster was incapable of speaking below a roar) set fire to the debris of a stable some distance from the old town. The fire spread to a nearby hay field and then swept over the town's remaining buildings, and soon nothing but ashes were left to mark where the saucy pioneer community had stood.

Islanders watched it burn, perhaps only half aware that an era was passing. For now San Juan had, or soon would have, a county seat, many stores, prosperous farms and fisheries, boat-building and other industries, established homes and families, regular steamer service, a telegraph, a newspaper.

For San Juan Island, at least, the pioneer days were gone forever.

Chapter Five

Friday Harbor, the County Seat

*A*ccording to a popular story, Friday Harbor was named by accident when a government survey vessel nosed into the bay there in the late 1850s. A Hawaiian sheepherder stood on the shore, watching. An officer on the survey boat, supposing the local people had some sort of name for the harbor, called out: "What bay is this?" The Kanaka, so they say, thought he asked "What *day* is this?"

"Friday," he called back to the boat, and the survey officer wrote on the map: Friday Bay.

This is one of those charming stories that are more fiction than fact, but there is at least a kernel of truth in it, as the town was certainly named for–if not by–an early resident, a Kanaka, who had been brought to the island by the Hudson's Bay Company to herd sheep.

The Kanaka's name was Joseph Pa'ilie (the spelling is uncertain), but everyone called him Joe Friday. He used to graze his flocks on the broad, grassy banks extending from Point Caution, where the Marine Laboratories are now, to the present town site. He had a shack or tent of some sort near the water's edge where, old-timers recalled, "his was the only smoke to be seen on that side of the island."

Early boatsmen used to steer by that smoke, and the snug bay was popularly called Friday's harbor.

When the town was laid out in 1875, the name was kept intact, including the possessive, and the earliest maps in the county courthouse are said to have shown it that way. Later the *'s* was dropped and the name has remained Friday Harbor to this day.

Another often-heard story about the town's name is probably less apocryphal than the one about the survey boat. It seems the post office once delivered a letter, postmarked on a Saturday, addressed by some wag to a friend at "Yesterday Harbor."

San Juan County was created by the Washington Legislature shortly after the boundary settlement in 1872. Captain Edward S.

"Dickie" Warbass and other pioneers looked about for a place to establish a county seat and soon decided on the present site because of its fine harbor and central location. They took advantage of a law permitting a county to claim open land, much as settlers filed homestead claims, and a quarter section was thus staked and filed for, before a single building had been erected anywhere in the vicinity.

Friday Harbor continued to be more theory than fact for the first couple of years. The place was awarded a post office, but it did little business. Ed Warbass took to riding horseback to San Juan Town and mailing letters to himself–otherwise, like as not, the mail boat wouldn't even stop at Friday Harbor.

Warbass himself lived just outside of town in the little building, said to be the first lumber-built house on the island, that had been Captain Pickett's. Warbass purchased it and had it moved to his waterfront claim.

The only road in town so far was the sheep trail which led from the waterfront to the spring–the one for which Spring Street is named–in the middle of town.

The spring was a copious one which served as a community watering place. It was some years before a more modern water supply and pipeline were installed, after which the spring continued to flow as abundantly as before, causing all sorts of problems. A pipe was eventually buried under Spring Street all the way to the bay to divert the water. Even so, buildings near the spring all have shallow foundations, and none have basements, because of seepage from the town's first water supply.

The spring is located under the intersection of Spring and Second Street opposite the drugstore. Only a slight depression in the paving marks the spot today.

Warbass believed Friday Harbor would have a great future (he foresaw a day when boats would enter and leave the bay every five minutes) but in its first decade the town remained pretty much of a dud. Only after two stores and, more significantly perhaps, two saloons opened in town did Friday Harbor finally begin to grow.

San Juan Island had had telegraph communication with the outside world as far back as 1866 when cables were laid under the water linking the island with both Victoria and the American

*Dr. V. G. Capron,
pioneer physician on San
Juan Island and founder
of the Island Telephone Co.*

mainland. The pioneer settler, Charles McKay, sent the first civilian message over the line–at a cost of $30.50.

The Island Telephone Company (later Inter-Island Telephone Co.) was established in 1900 by Dr. V. G. Capron, a forward looking citizen who was also responsible for the town's first electric plant and other innovations–including a portable x-ray machine he invented and used in his country practice. Capron lived in Roche Harbor and had an office in Friday Harbor; the phone system began as a single line linking the two places. By 1901 the system had spread to 33 subscribers scattered around the island, and some 25 miles of wire had been strung.

Talking on the phone wasn't cheap. Rates were $2.50 a month for a place on the party line–twice that for businesses–and when cables were laid between the islands in 1904, it cost 40 cents a minute just to talk from San Juan to Orcas, 50 cents to Bellingham, and 60 cents a minute to Seattle, quite considerable sums in those days.

By this time the old military telegraph cable had long been out of commission due to deterioration in the salt water. It was never replaced. However in 1903 the Pacific Wireless Telegraph Company set up a radio station near the present courthouse site and built a powerful Marconi spark transmitter, said to be the most potent on the American continent except for Marconi's own station at St. John's, Newfoundland.

The company intended the station to be a relay point for their Alaska business and in order to get as strong a signal on the air as possible they built a 200-foot-high wooden mast–the highest such mast in the world, according to the company.

The distinction was short-lived.

The station went on the air February 10, 1904, just as a winter windstorm was gathering itself for a good southeast blow. Operators H. A. Yarnell and DeBault had sent and received a few inaugural messages when there was a deafening report like a cannon shot, and the raspy dash-dot sounds in their earphones quit abruptly.

DeBault and Yarnell rushed outside in time to see the top 80 feet of the "world's tallest wooden mast" come crashing to the earth, carrying with it most of the guy wires, and buckling the huge concrete blocks in which the base had been imbedded.

The wireless company decided to move the station to the top of Bald Hill, a few miles east of town, where they wouldn't need a mast quite that high.

Wireless messages to Seattle cost 50 cents for ten words and three cents for each additional word.

Electricity first flowed in Friday Harbor on January 5, 1907. The first arc lamp was suspended across Spring Street at the town's main corner. Apparently technical problems plagued the new venture, for the Friday Harbor Journal editorialized on the fifteenth of August: "The electric lights are as spasmodic as 'chills and fever'–good for a few moments, and very poor for half an evening or more. If the cause of their being good once in a while could be discovered, and the art made permanent use of, there would be cause for congratulations."

There were no congratulations the following week, however, when the Journal reported the light company's steam-operated dynamo had been "stealthily removed from the plant" in the middle of the night, leaving the town without any lights at all, spasmodic or otherwise.

Today the Islands' electric power is supplied by an REA cooperative, the Orcas Power and Light Company, popularly known as OPALCO. The company maintains an office and substation on San Juan, but its main plant is on Orcas. Power comes from the mainland by a system of underwater high-voltage cables, a technique pioneered by the co-op. OPALCO's first cross-sound cable, when laid in 1951, was the world's longest.

The early cables failed periodically, while the more conventional overhead power lines in these heavily-wooded islands were easily downed by windstorms. Orcas Power and Light Company's outages were so common, islanders jokingly called it the "Occasional" Power and Light Co.*

Today with back-up cables in place at each crossing, and much of the overland wiring undergrounded, the San Juans' utilities are almost as dependable as those on the mainland. Still, wintertime sees prudent islanders stocking up on flashlights and long-johns, kerosene lamps and firewood–just in case.

Friday Harbor has had a newspaper since 1890 when Frank P. Baum established the San Juan Graphic there. The Graphic had a short existence and was followed in 1891 by the San Juan Islander, which had a succession of editors until 1895 when two brothers, Otis and Fred Culver, took it over.

The Culvers, who were strong Republicans, never hesitated to express their political views in the vivid manner customary of the journals and journalists of that period. When some years later a division arose in the county's Republican party, O. G. Wall and G. A. Ludwig formed a company and began publishing the Friday Harbor Journal in political opposition to the Islander. The first issue of the Journal was printed September 13, 1906.

The next year a new partner came into the Journal enterprise. He was Virgil Frits, 24-year-old son of a pioneer Orcas family, who had learned his trade as a printer on newspapers in Bellingham and

*The Inter-Island Telephone Co., similarly outage-plagued, was likewise dubbed the "Intermittent" phone company.

*Otis H. Culver
publisher of the early
newspaper the San Juan
Islander. Culver was also
Collector of Customs at
Roche Harbor*

Seattle. "Virge" took over as editor soon afterward, thus beginning a career that would last half a century and make him a legend in the San Juans.

The Journal's beef with the Islander was that publisher O. H. Culver had sold out to the county's political boss, Roche Harbor lime magnate John S. McMillin. Moreover, Culver was simultaneously drawing pay from the federal government as Collector of Customs–a patronage job Frits and others considered a form of payoff–and was even charging Uncle Sam rent for his own office in the Islander building. Frits waged such effective journalistic war over these and other issues that the Islander simply passed out of existence a few years later on.

The Journal settled into being a folksy little paper filled largely with social notes of the "Mr. and Mrs. Sam Jones spent Thursday of last week on the mainland" variety. Frits did most of the work himself, passing long hours at the linotype machine, a well-chewed cigar–usually cold–clamped firmly in a kindly face that smiled much and spoke little. The Journal's small shop on Spring Street,* delightfully cluttered and redolent of hot lead and ink, with its dim lighting and smoky wood stove, and with pictures on the wall of just about every Republican that ever ran for President--successfully or not--was where townspeople gathered to pass along or catch up on the local news, or just to kill time.

Virge's wife Maude would most likely be found at the desk by the window, collecting subscriptions and want-ads, processing the scribbled news notes people dropped by with, and deflecting the conversation of visitors so Virge could get on with the work.

Fiscally and politically conservative and staunchly anti-union, Frits wrote editorials that sometimes bordered on the inflammatory. Once following a nasty incident elsewhere in the state in which a union demonstrator wound up lynched, Frits defended the action, writing that in such instances "mob violence...is the only course to take." The county prosecutor called this inciting to violence and charged Frits with criminal libel. Most in the county shared the editor's views, however, and after a brief trial it took a jury of Frits' peers all of five minutes to find him not guilty.

Frits is probably remembered more for his pithy one-line observations, sometimes used as "fillers" at the end of a column, like: "The abolition of the woodshed, as heating plants come into general use, in our opinion may have serious effects upon the education of children." Still he never took himself too seriously either, one day penning: "If you agree with everything the editor says, you have no more sense than the editor."

Under Frits, the paper never was late, and never missed an issue. You could set your clock by the roar of the old Cottrell cylinder press each Wednesday, which was also the signal for generations of Friday Harbor youngsters to come by after school and earn pocket money helping to hand-fold the freshly printed papers. Kids were rewarded with $2 each and supper until state government grinches ended the tradition, claiming it violated child labor laws.

Bob and Mildred Hartzog took over the Journal when Frits retired in 1958, and apart from some mechanical improvements,

*The building is now National Park headquarters.

*Virgil Frits, legendary country editor of
the Friday Harbor Journal*

ran it in pretty much the same countrified way Frits had done. After Hartzog died in 1969, however, a series of new publishers and editors have made many changes, including the name (it's the Journal of the San Juans now), a new location and new, modern equipment, and a more liberal political stance that would no doubt have Virgil Frits chomping his cigar in fury.

After the Islander's demise around 1914, the Journal had no further competition until the late sixties when it was challenged by the Orcas-based Islands' Sounder, founded by Al Magnuson. The Sounder had been a free, irregularly-appearing promotional sheet until its gradual transformation into a paid county-wide news weekly. Lopez at one time fielded a highly readable but short-lived rival paper of its own, the Island Record, and currently offers a free shopper-type weekly which no doubt has higher aspirations.

Today, the Journal and Sounder are both absentee-owned, multisectioned newspapers, heavy with photos and features and trying hard to look and read like their sophisticated mainland cousins.

Only two or three other businesses in the Islands date back as far as the Journal. The San Juan County Bank, established in Friday Harbor in 1893 with a capital stock of $15,000, is now (with branches on Orcas and Lopez) part of Key Bank of Washington. Just as Virgil Frits personified the Friday Harbor Journal for so long, the bank was virtually synonymous with its long-time president, Cecil L. Carter. Carter was still a teenager when he began his career there, joining the bank back in 1907 as (so he recalled it) "janitor and bookkeeper."

For most of the years since, the Bank occupied the squarish building on Friday Harbor's main corner. The building probably kept most of the town from burning to the ground in 1943 when a fire razed nearly everything from First Street to the bay, stopping only at the bank's concrete and brick.

The Friday Harbor Drug Company is another pioneer enterprise that has continued to the present day. It was established before the turn of the century and acquired in 1902 by Dr. George S. Wright, the county coroner. Leon Little, a cousin of Dr. Wright's, and Albert Nash, Sr. operated it for some years.

In 1920, Little and Nash acquired the property southeast of town which had been the claim of Friday Harbor founder Ed Warbass. Warbass had called his place "Idlewild," but Little and Nash turned it into a resort–the island's first–and renamed it Kwan Lamah. The words are Chinook Jargon for "glad" and "hand," hence "welcome."

The Little-Nash partnership was dissolved a few years later with the Little family continuing to operate Kwan Lamah, and Al Nash devoting his full time to the drugstore. Today his son, Al Jr., continues to run this long-time institution.

For many years Al Jr. was chairman of the committee that put on the town's big annual celebration known as the San Juan Rendezvous. The Rendezvous was originally intended as a summer-time attraction for pleasure boaters. Huge quantities of barbecued salmon, salad and coffee were served free of charge to visitors, with local folks digging up donations to pay for the eats. After the first affair was held in 1948, however, as word got around the crowds grew bigger and the town had to begin levying a modest charge per plate.

Currently it's the Pig War Barbecue, held the third Saturday in June of each year, that attracts throngs of visitors from around the Northwest–and with scant need to advertise the event!

Even greater crowds besiege the island the last full weekend of July to attend the renowned San Juan Island Dixieland Jazz Festival. This swinging affair draws upwards of a dozen top bands from all over the nation, playing in various venues around the town, to fans in their thousands who crowd planes, ferries and private boats to get to where this action is. Hotel and motel rooms sell out 'way in advance, campsites are maxed, and even sleeping bag space can get hard to find. Washington State Ferries adds extra sailings on Festival weekends, with morning and evening boats packed out by jazz-loving daytrippers.

Another popular attraction in Friday Harbor is the unique Whale Museum, housed unpretentiously in the town's erstwhile Odd Fellows Hall. Displays tell you everything you want to know about whales, especially the so-called "killer whales" or orcas which inhabit local waters. The Museum is a nationally recognized center that attracts whale researchers from around the world. If you wish to see live orcas disporting themselves in their natural element, you need only go to Lime Kiln Point State Park, a few miles away. A little luck is needed too, as the three resident whale pods, or families, keep to their own schedule and may or may not appear when you would like. But this is the world's only whale watching park, and you're as likely to see orcas here as anywhere.

Another unique research center is the Friday Harbor Marine Laboratories, operated by the University of Washington and attended by advanced students of the University's departments of oceanography, zoology, meteorology, botany, and fisheries. The Laboratories, formerly known as the Marine Station and later as the Puget Sound Biological Station,* were first established at Friday Harbor in 1903 by the University's prominent biologist, Professor Trevor Kincaid. He and Dr. Theodore C. Frye, who stayed on as director of the facility for many years, were the whole faculty when classes were first held in 1904.

The students really roughed it those first years, living in

*Islanders call it the "bug station."

unfloored tents and doing their studying and research out in the open.

Andrew Newhall donated three acres of his property–near Warbass' Idlewild–for a permanent camp in 1909 and the school was held there for some years. The original laboratory building still stands, barely above high tide line, perched on stilt-like pilings just east of town. Above it on the hill was erected a large dining hall, around which were the tents which served as dormitories for students and faculty.

In 1922 the federal government donated to the University the property now occupied by the Laboratories north of town. This was the old Point Caution military preserve, or "Indian Reserve" as the early settlers called it. The 484 acres, with plenty of varied waterfront, fireproof buildings, a fine research library, and modern laboratory equipment are the realization of the earliest dreams of the marine facility's founders.

Ed Warbass' dream of vessels entering and leaving Joe Friday's bay every few minutes has also been realized–at least it is on most summer days–but not quite in the way he imagined. It's not commerce but pleasure that brings the parade of ferries, yachts, cruisers and kicker-boats into port. The principal business in this town, apart from real estate and construction companies, is now a burgeoning county government which has long since outgrown the little red-brick 1906-built courthouse just up from the drugstore.

Friday Harbor may still *look* like a thirties-era town driven by fishing and agriculture, but its real industries today are growth and tourism. The challenge now for this town that almost never started is how to keep its growing popularity from destroying the very ambience people come here to enjoy.

Chapter Six

Roche Harbor: the Town That Lime Built

7 hough the economy of the San Juans over the years has been based on activities as diverse as farming, fishing, logging, fruit-growing and tourism, the single most important source of income historically has been: LIME. Crude early-day lime quarries put coins in the pockets of islanders with no other way of making a living, or bolstered the income of families living on small farms. For scores of years it was next to impossible to starve in the San Juan Islands, because there was always wood to be cut for a dollar and a quarter a cord at the lime companies. Many residents had one way of earning a living in the summertime–fishing, for instance–and another in the winter, when the kilns' appetite for wood was, if anything, even greater.

The old kilns were generally made as great stone towers and some can still be seen today, perched along the water's edge perhaps, or standing solitary watch over some deserted inland glade, surrounded by second-growth trees and scrub brush. A dozen or so of these old kilns, some of them reduced to mere heaps of rubble, can be found still on Orcas Island. Seven still stand on San Juan, one on Crane, and two are still to be seen on Henry Island.

On San Juan's west side, Lime Kiln Lighthouse was named for what is supposed to be the first kiln in the Islands. Operated by Augustus Hibbard during the 1860s, the enterprise was dogged by trouble and tragedy. Quarrymen were suspected of bootlegging whiskey to Indians and soldiers. Hibbard's cook was stabbed to death in one altercation and Hibbard himself was killed in another, involving an Indian woman.

A successor came out from the East to take the operation over and he, too, was dead in less than three years.

Early kilns on Orcas Island were established at Langdon, on the eastern shore of East Sound, and along the island's west coast.

British soldiers during Pig War days are credited with shipping the first lime from the island. It was quarried by hand, burned in old-fashioned pot kilns and shipped to Victoria in empty whiskey kegs.

After the British left the island the property on which their primitive kilns are supposed to have stood was homesteaded by Joe Ruff. Ruff sold out around 1880 to two brothers, Robert and Richard Scurr. The Scurrs operated the quarries on the north end of the island for a few years, but in a small way.

In 1886 there entered upon the scene a dynamic man whose rugged individualism and personal electricity were to influence the Islands' development–and dominate their politics–for many decades to come. John Stafford McMillin, a Midwesterner, a lawyer, above all an astute businessman and steadfast Republican, left his mark on the San Juans as no other man before or since.

McMillin had been for several years associated with the Tacoma Lime Works. In the 1880s he came to the Islands to look for properties the company could profitably acquire, and he quickly realized the tremendous potential of the Roche Harbor quarries. For here was a ledge of the purest limestone, a quarter of a mile wide and three-quarters of a mile long, extending from the waterline across the tip of San Juan to Westcott Bay. The supply was considered inexhaustible.

The harbor itself was perfectly suited for a major industry, as its abundant deep waters, well protected by Pearl and Henry Islands, were ideal for even the largest ocean-going craft.

The property was purchased in 1886 and the Tacoma and Roche Harbor Lime Company was formed. McMillin threw all his energy into the enterprise which quickly became a thriving business, of which John S. was soon elevated to the presidency.

McMillin took every advantage of the limestone's convenient location above the harbor. Quarries were opened on high ground where the stone could be loaded on small cars which descended a slight grade to the kilns. There were two batteries of kilns–thirteen in all–including eleven massive steel kilns of the most modern type.

Burned lime was withdrawn at a lower level by means of chutes leading directly into the barreling rooms. When filled and weighed, the barrels were trucked the short distance to the huge waterfront warehouse, whose stowing capacity was 20,000 barrels.

The company had its own fleet of vessels, including the brig *William G. Irwin,* the steam tug *Roche Harbor,* and five barges.

John S. McMillin
Controversial President of the
Roche Harbor Lime & Cement Co.

By 1890 the lime company had built an industry that supported a town of 247 residents. It was a company town in the full sense of the word, as were many–if not most–one-industry towns in America during that period. Every building on the 4,000-acre empire was erected, owned, and administered by the company. No business enterprises but the company's were allowed. Employees and their families were "encouraged"–a stronger word might be even more correct–to trade only at the company store, live in company-owned rental cottages, relax in the company's saloon, pray in the company's church, and be buried in the company's cemetery.

Still it is only fair to say that the company provided incomes, over the years, to thousands of people; that the company loyally looked after the interests of its workers, so long as the employees were equally loyal to the company; that the company was far and away San Juan County's major generator of income, whose presence benefitted not just that island, but the rest of the county as well.

Many tales are told supposedly proving the company ruled

tyrannically over the lives and souls of its employees, but for every such story there is another, telling of some act of kindness or assistance performed by the company or its officers to a worker in need.

In a few years Roche Harbor had become the largest lime producer west of the Mississippi. Its product, important for agriculture and for making cement and other products, was considered the purest available. Roche Harbor lime was widely exported to the Orient and South America, besides enjoying a thriving business in the States.

Mrs. McMillin was largely responsible for the town's beautification project which continued all the years the company was in business. Scow-loads of sandstone boulders were brought in from Lopez and Stuart Islands to make a seawall, corresponding to the present waterfront. For years the area between it and the road was a dumping ground for core lime, a waste product. Upon this fill were placed huge quantities of topsoil brought from Westcott Bay. Then beautiful gardens were laid out and landscaped with great care under the personal supervision of the McMillins. The colorful gardens reaching to the water's edge were one of the first sights to greet the eyes of visitors arriving by boat in the harbor.

McMillin loved the town and delighted in showing it off. He often brought whole boatloads of business acquaintances to the island for a weekend of entertainment, fine food, and country living. Visitors were put up in the historic Hotel de Haro, built in 1886 around the sturdy log bunkhouse erected by Hudson's Bay for Kanakas herding sheep there.

Next to the hotel the company built gigantic barbecue courts with two huge outdoor fireplaces. The courts were attractively decorated with flower beds, flower boxes, and potted plants and were covered with trellises of Virginia Creeper and trained Clematis. There was a pergola leading from the hotel, through the gardens, to the waterfront. Filipino waiters in white uniforms attended to visitors at the hotel or escorted them to and from the harbor.

John S. McMillin quickly became the most powerful man in the Islands, his penchant for politics showing itself soon after the establishment of the company in Roche Harbor. By 1905 it was

The Roche Harbor waterfront in its heyday

noted he'd been a member of "every territorial, county, and state convention of the Republican party" since coming to the island. The same year (1905) he was appointed railway commissioner by Washington's Governor Mead.

In 1906 McMillin made a deal to sell the Roche Harbor company to an Eastern group, but was blocked by a court injunction from completing the sale when minority stockholders accused him of fraud and "questionable transactions" in the running of the company's affairs. The case, which was heard by Judge Hanford in Seattle, dragged on for two years but in the end McMillin was fully vindicated.

The San Juan Islander, which sometimes championed McMillin and at other times accused "the president of the lime kiln club" of political bossism, devoted almost its whole front page to the story of the suit's outcome. In the same issue the news of the death of President Cleveland was given a one-column box only two and a half inches long.

The suit was still pending during the elections of 1906, the year of the Republican split, when a rump party of independent Republicans ran successfully against the McMillin-backed candidates. The rumps, which called themselves the "Independent Manhood of San Juan County," even carried Roche Harbor precinct–by three votes.

In spite of the outcome of the fraud case, McMillin's political and business future was surely checked by the adverse publicity. Accused of having used his appointment as railroad commissioner to obtain preferential rates for his company, he resigned that position. The lime company sale was canceled, and his dream of running for Congress was never to come true either. McMillin spent the rest of his life on San Juan Island, devoting most of his time to the company and to his family–and making good his vow to see that his stockholders never got another dime in dividends.

In 1923 a great fire swept over the Roche Harbor waterfront, destroying the lime plant, warehouses, store, dock, and other buildings. Afterwards the building which now serves the boatel complex as its restaurant was erected for the McMillins as their official residence. For their private lives, however, McMillin built another home on a high, remote wooded hill north of town. He called the place with its sylvan surroundings "Afterglow Manor."

A special family pleasure was to linger about the dinner table in the evenings, watching the sun go down in flames behind the Canadian islands across Haro Strait.

In the thirties McMillin designed and built a family mausoleum at Afterglow Manor. It still stands, and besides being the final resting place of the McMillins, has become a tourist attraction. The monument consists of a circle of seven 30-foot Tuscan columns joined at the top in a crown-like ring. Under the columns is a raised platform, in the center of which are a round table and six chairs cast in cement.

Leading up to the platform are three tiers of stairs. On the riser of the first stair is the name: *McMillin.* The first tier consists of three steps, the second five, and the third seven, with short landings between tiers.

Around the table the chairs are spaced at equal intervals, except that between two of the chairs there is an extra space, as though another chair were missing.

Behind the "missing chair" one of the Tuscan columns is incomplete, as though it had been broken away.

The symbolism of the monument has fired the imagination of many visitors. A popular notion is that the broken column and the missing chair represent an anonymous "black sheep" of the family. Another story is that the open space between the columns and chairs allows the rays of the sun to strike the center of the table at a certain hour on an annual date which has some family significance.

Actually the broken column is intended to represent life broken by death, and the ring at the top signifies eternal life after death. There is no missing chair. The space was left on the west side because the family used to sit that way around their dinner table so no one would have his back to the view.

Besides, the space on the west side makes the chair on the east–McMillin's own–the head of the table. That's the only way this can be accomplished, of course, with a round table.

Some elements of the symbolism are recognizable by Freemasons. McMillin was a Knight Templar.

The mausoleum was finished in the spring of 1936. In November of that same year John S. McMillin was himself the first to be laid to rest there. As he had intended, his ashes were inurned in the concrete chair inscribed with his name.

Mrs. Luella Hiett McMillin died in 1943, and her ashes were inurned there as well. Sons John, Fred, and Paul, and one daughter, Dorothy, are also there in chairs bearing their names. Each of the

children was given the middle name Hiett, Mrs. McMillin's maiden name.

By the mid-1950s the lime supply that had been thought "inexhaustible" had played out and Paul, last of the McMillin sons, sold the company–town, mausoleum and all–to Reuben Tarte of Seattle. Tarte, a boating enthusiast, and his family set about transforming Roche Harbor into a tourist mecca that today offers many modern amenities while still preserving an aura of bygone times. Moorage for pleasure boats of all sizes, a gas dock and grocery store are available year-around. There are miles of wooded trails to hike and explore, along with a good airstrip, a popular restaurant, swimming pool, beauty shop, post office and so on.

The old Hotel de Haro has been completely rebuilt inside, while the exterior has been restored to look just about as it did a century ago. President Theodore Roosevelt was a guest here once in 1906, staying in room 10. "Teddy's" signature used to be on display in the lobby register–until somebody stole it. President Taft is also said to have stayed at the De Haro, which today is on the National Register of Historic Places.

The home the McMillins called Afterglow Manor burned down on Memorial Day, 1944. All that is left there is a pile of stones and a few charred beams. The lime that built the town and fueled an era is gone as well. But Roche Harbor remains, secure in its history and great natural beauty, a perennial attraction for boaters and landsmen alike.

51

Orcas—the "Mystic" Isle

O rcas is the largest of the San Juans, edging out San Juan Island for this honor by a single square mile of area. Shaped like a pair of huge saddle bags, the island's wasp-waste–extending from the head of East Sound to North Beach–is so low that, if the level of the sea were to rise another ten feet, Orcas would become two separate islands.

Because of its shape Orcas has an extensive shoreline, scalloped with innumerable small bays and quiet coves, which has made the island especially popular with tourists for many decades. Orcas has the largest number of resorts in the archipelago (but by no means all of them) and, apart from the real estate and construction businesses, tourism is the island's chief industry.

Mary and Pat Norton are credited with starting the resort business in the San Juans about 1910. The Nortons boarded some schoolteacher friends at their Deer Harbor farm that year; the next year the teachers wanted to come back with some of their friends. So Mary ordered canvas out of a mail-order catalog, stitched some tents together, and the family was in the resort business.

Even before Norton's Inn was established, Luther Sutherland was hosting paying guests in elegant fashion at East Sound House, which he built around the original log building erected there by the pioneer, Charles Shattuck. The hotel, enlarged and still going strong, is known today as the Outlook Inn.

The very earliest record of summer resorting on Orcas is found in the memoirs of a pioneer islander who recalled that in the 1860s and '70s, the shoreline at Crescent Beach was white with the tents of mainland people who had come over to the island to "get away from it all."

Even before this, the Indians used to come here from all up and down the coast to loaf, fish, dig clams, and enjoy life. So no one really knows when this business of summering on Orcas first started.

Indians were among the few regular customers of Paul Hubbs'

store at Grindstone Bay. When the store burned down sometime in the 1860s, Hubbs moved to San Juan Island. Captain Stephen Sweeney started a store soon afterward at what was then known as Sweeney Bay, a few hundred yards east of the present ferry dock. He applied for the first post office which, when awarded, was named Orcas Island.

Later Sweeney traded the store to a Mr. Edwards for a boat. Edwards subsequently sold the store to a Canadian, William E. Sutherland. Sutherland then moved the whole operation over to the site of today's ferry landing where he also built a wharf, storehouse, dancehall and hotel.

The Orcas Store has been rebuilt once or twice since then but is still very much in operation, as is the attractive hotel which dominates the hillside above. Now on the National Registry of historic buildings, the hotel today is downright sedate compared with its checkered past as a sometime haven for assorted smugglers and bootleggers, not to mention occasional women of doubtful virtue; as the site of at least one Wild-West style shootout; and where the ghost of the lady who ran the inn all through that colorful era is claimed to haunt the place even yet.

Another pioneer store, post office, and dance hall operation had been built by John Ohlert on the east side of the island, at a place he called Olga. (Olga was Ohlert's mother's name.) It was a popular spot to which people came from all around–by foot, horseback, and even rowboat–to attend the lively dances. The second-floor dance hall was partitioned into hotel rooms later on. The building, one of the oldest in the San Juans, was largely destroyed in a fire some years ago, but part was saved and remodeled into a private dwelling that still overlooks the Olga waterfront.

Olga today is a sleepy little village with a summertime-only general store, small rustic post office, and a popular cafe and co-op store where Island artists hang out and offer their wares for sale.

The largest town on Orcas, and second largest commercial center in the county, is Eastsound (one word) located at the head of the bay called East Sound (two words). This now bustling community boasts a supermarket-style grocery store, two banks, several fine restaurants, bookstores, a drug store, newspaper, performing arts center, craft and gift shops and art galleries and various other places of business. Gone from the town's main corner is historic Templin's, the picturesque country store where you could find anything from horse collars to wash tubs hanging from the ceiling, where the village elders gathered around a pot-bellied stove to discuss the weather, and you could get your coffee ground before your eyes in a big red hand-operated grinder. Templin's lives on, though, as a rambling mini-mall which incorporates the older store building.

Across from Templin's the little 1886-built Community Church is also gone, its members having erected a new and larger building—the one with the distinctive bell tower—up on Madrona Street. Contrasting with today's active congregation, there were just three members when the Rev. John Tennant founded the church in 1884. Tennant and his Indian wife only survived those first years by living on clams dug from the beach out front.

Just down the street is the island's oldest house of worship, Emmanuel Church, founded in 1885 by the Rev. Sidney R. S. Gray, who also drew the plans for the attractive building. Gray, who was from England and hoped to see Eastsound become the kind of rural

Historic Emmanuel Church, Eastsound

village he had known back home, styled the building as a typical English country church. The church's prime waterfront lot had originally been intended as the site for a saloon–indeed the foundation had already been prepared for it–but Gray and others mounted an unrelenting opposition that finally drove the would-be saloon-keeper from the island, and convinced the lot's owner to donate the land for the church instead.

It was Gray who encouraged local farmers to start the fruit-growing industry that brought Orcas a short-lived prosperity, and he himself platted an addition to Eastsound on nearby Madrona Point, which he proposed to call "Village de Haro." He even named the streets and drew up plans for two high class private schools for boys and girls. This dream went out the window, however, along with many others in the bank panic of 1893. Gray left the island not long afterward, and only then did his old friends and parishioners learn that Gray's gracious wife was of royal blood–the daughter of the sovereign of the German state of Mecklenburg-Schwerin.

Madrona Point, a gently-wooded 30-acre peninsula of great natural beauty, remained undeveloped over the years (except for one small resort operation) until the mid-1980s when a developers' conglomerate bought it and announced plans to carve it into homesites and apartment complexes. As bulldozers prepared to roll, Bellingham's Lummi Indians came forward to claim the Point was sacred land in their tradition, and should be left alone. Archaeologists found no burial sites, but citizen groups and even the Greater Seattle Church Council supported the Lummis' view that the Point was somehow special. Congress finally stepped in with funds enabling the Lummis to buy Madrona Point and keep it pristine.

Actually it's not just Native Americans for whom Orcas holds spiritual, if not downright mystical attractions. Camp Indralaya (often referred to by locals as "the T. S. Camp") has been a gathering place for devotees of Theosophical Society teachings since 1927. The Louis Foundation–whose founder claims to have clairvoyant powers in the tradition of Edgar Cayce–numbers many seekers after the occult among patrons of historic Outlook Inn, which it has owned and operated for the past thirty years. Other groups preoccupied with New Age spirituality keep popping up as

Peaceful Madrona Point

well, including followers of J. Z. Knight's "Ramtha" channeling, whose publishing house was based at Eastsound for a time.

On an even more arcane level, perhaps, are those who are seriously convinced fairies inhabit Mount Constitution, and that supernatural energy "vortices" in and around Orcas make this a magical island in the literal, and not just the figurative sense.

Most Orcas dwellers today, however, are down-to-earth as were their predecessors, the hardy pioneers whose hand-hewn log cabins once dotted the local forests. As for the cabins, few still stand–though one serves as an eye-catching roadside shop for ceramics, souvenirs and so on in Crow Valley. Several of the earliest ones have been salvaged and moved to Eastsound, where they have been joined together to form a unique kind of historical museum for the safe-keeping of old records, pictures, and other relics. The project is under the auspices of the Orcas Island Historical Society, whose members don period costumes during the summer tourist season to act as guides and answer questions at the museum.

Here one can see displayed reminders of the San Juans' earliest days: Pig War cannon balls; a pioneer doctor's curious medical kit; Indian artifacts and some that may be pre-Indian; the handmade rowboat in which Ethan Allen, the county's turn-of-the-century school superintendent, rowed thousands of miles doing his job of keeping contact with the many little country schools scattered around the islands.

Most of all, the museum serves as a portrayal of the hardness of pioneer life on this frontier, and moreover, that this kind of life was being lived here on the islands more recently than we might otherwise think.

No one in the Historical Society (much less the island's supposed psychics) has the answer, now, to Orcas Island's mysterious "anchor." This enigmatic marker is found high on the top of Turtleback Mountain, the 1500-foot hill opposite Waldron Island on Orcas' west coast. On a grassy slope near Turtleback's

Historical Museum at Eastsound, Orcas Island

highest point there is carefully laid out in rocks twice the size of a man's fist a replica of the kind of anchor used on sailing vessels in the old, old days of the square-riggers.

Who put it there, and why, is a mystery about which there are many theories, but few facts. The oldest inhabitants assure us it has been there as long as there have been white settlers on Orcas.

An old newspaper still extant tells us the same thing. It is also claimed traces of a wrecked sailing ship from the period in question were found long ago on the rocks off Steep Point, not far from Turtleback. Thus one theory holds that an early exploring ship was wrecked there and the men who survived, knowing it might be many long years before others passed the same way, left the anchor to show seafaring men had once lived there.

A possibly related tale about Turtleback–this one documented by a contemporary newspaper account–chronicles the landing on Orcas in November, 1903, of four men described as "swarthy foreigners" speaking a strange language, one of whom was an old man "upwards of 90" whose "tottering steps two of the younger men supported." The old man directed his companions to a large moss-covered boulder which they overturned, and under which they found a black bottle. Compass bearings were taken from this point and the men disappeared up the side of Turtleback, returning the next day to their boat, in which they sailed off to the north.

Some accounts say the "swarthy foreigners" took a chest (full of treasure, of course) with them when they left, while others say they dug holes all over Turtleback but didn't find any chest, in which case the treasure–if any–is presumably still there.

Orcas Island's Turtleback Mountain

Chapter Eight

Rosario and Mount Constitution

*A*bout the time Turtleback's mysterious visitors did or did not remove a great treasure from Orcas, another man–no foreigner to the Pacific Northwest–was preparing to spend his own fortune on the island. This was the fabulous Robert Moran, twice mayor of Seattle, builder of great naval ships and Yukon River flatboats, a self-made man risen from humble origins to become one of Puget Sound's leading industrialists.

Moran had probably never heard of Orcas Island when he first landed at Yesler's Wharf in Seattle one rainy November morning in 1875. The young lad from the New York City tenements had followed Horace Greely's advice to "go west" and here he was, without relatives or friends, with no job and no prospects, strolling up the pioneer town's Front Street with a single thin dime in his pocket, in search of breakfast.

Moran picked up the scent of eggs and flapjacks and followed it to an eatery known as Our House, run by a black man named Bill Gross. Gross staked the youngster to a meal on credit and told him about a logging camp across Lake Washington that was looking for a cook. Moran's instincts were all in the mechanical rather than the culinary line, but a job was a job, and he took it.

Moran lasted three days as a cook, and earned just enough to buy a pair of shoes, to replace the ones he wore out walking back to Seattle from the logging camp.

Before long Moran found work on a steamboat, the old sidewheeler *J. B. Libby,* as a deckhand. The *Libby* carried mail between Seattle and Bellingham, and thus did the boy from New York–who had just turned eighteen–get his first good look at the San Juans.

Moran saved his money and in a short time had enough to marry his Canadian sweetheart, and to send for his mother, brothers, and sisters to join him.

A few more years and his savings came to $1600, with which capital he opened a marine repair shop on Yesler's Wharf. The enterprise had grown to a $40,000 business by 1889, when the great Seattle fire wiped it all out. There was no insurance, for the fire had destroyed the insurance company, too.

Still there was no stopping Bob Moran, who rebuilt his plant and entered the shipbuilding business. His greatest achievement–aside from overseeing, as mayor, Seattle's rebuilding after the fire–was constructing the first-class battleship *Nebraska*, far and away the largest vessel to be built on Puget Sound at that time.

It was Moran's passion for hard work, his doctors believed, that brought about his physical collapse in 1904. They gave him six months to live. So Moran sold his Seattle shipyard and retired to Orcas Island where he went to work just as hard as before, building a palatial home and improving the thousands of acres of property he acquired nearby.

The core of Moran's estate was purchased from Andrew Newhall and his associates, whose mills on Cascade Bay had been producing lumber, boxes, and barrels for Orcas Island's lime works. There were a number of residents, several buildings and even a post office at the little community then known as Newhall. Moran changed the name to Rosario, after the broad strait that separates the Islands from the mainland to the east.

Newhall removed his mill and box works, and Moran set about replacing them with newer equipment, including electric lights, a hydroelectric plant, and a machine shop.

Moran himself designed the mansion that was to become the family's home, and supervised its building. The house is one of the construction marvels of the Pacific Northwest. The foundation was literally blasted out of solid bedrock. The first two floors are made of concrete; only the third floor is of frame construction. The roof is composed of copper sheets weighing some six tons.

In the basement Moran built a swimming pool, billiard tables, and two bowling alleys–all embedded in the rock on which the house was built. A later owner offered to give the billiard tables away to a man who showed up with a truck to get them, only to discover they were impossible to move.

Upstairs Moran never settled for less than the best, and never followed traditional practices when he could think of something better. The interior doors were handmade, and used lignum vitae non-squeaking hinges invented by Moran. Windows, made of glass nearly an inch thick, were set directly into the concrete without frames.

Nearly all the hardware and wood trim were fashioned in Moran's own shops by top craftsmen. The parquet flooring and much of the mansion's interior finish is of teakwood, imported from the South Seas. The floor alone took two years to lay.

On the main floor is a massive fireplace made of concrete with bits of tile embedded in it. The tile is said to have come from Seattle's old Union Depot.

Upstairs is a huge music room surrounded by the pipes of a gigantic organ–it cost $30,000 originally and is worth many times that today–flanked by balconies on which are located the organ's console and two libraries. There is a beautiful stained glass window, protected by specially designed shutters, showing the harbor in Antwerp, Belgium. The window was imported from Brussels.

Moran was a music-lover. When he had guests in the house–and he had lots of guests, many of them in the Very Important Person category–he would waken them at 7 each morning with an organ concert. They would come to the floor

The Moran mansion, now Rosario Resort on Orcas Island

below and see Moran at the balcony console and, as the music poured majestic and flawless around them, marvel at the extent of this man's talents.

What they didn't know was that Moran wasn't really playing. The organ had been fitted with special equipment to play paper rolls, like a player piano. Few ever learned this secret.

Moran also built houses for other members of the family at Rosario and spruced up the estate by building a decorative 360-foot pool, paved streets, boat landings and the like. He put in street lights that are reminiscent of Seattle's in the early days. For his wife he built a unique "round house" of wedge-shaped rooms equipped for her own personal canning and baking activities.

In 1915 Moran went to San Juan Island and there salvaged the figurehead from a wrecked sailing ship, the *America,* intending to use it on a yacht he was planning to build for himself. Later he changed his mind and set the figurehead upon the lawn fronting the harbor, where it can still be seen. The *America* was one of the last of the clipper ships, and the figurehead–carved from a solid white pine log back in 1874, just a year before Moran left New York to seek his fortune in the West–is in a remarkably good state of preservation.

Moran's yacht, the *Sanwan,* was a triumph of construction, but his pleasure was in the building rather than the sailing of her, and he rarely ventured to sea in the yacht.

For many years Moran–always proud of the showplace he had built–devoted one day a week to showing it to the public. He usually acted as guide himself. The weekly open house ended abruptly, though, when a woman visitor was discovered one day taking a bath in Mrs. Moran's private tub.

During the first years Moran was on Orcas he had agents quietly buying up tracts of land surrounding Rosario. By 1921 he owned all of Mount Constitution except for one farm, which he was never able to buy, and with this exception offered the whole mountain to the State for a park. State officials were reluctant to accept the gift at first, but Moran twisted a few arms and today Moran State Park is one of Washington's most frequented, with its vast areas of untouched forest and protected wild life, lakes, streams, wooded trails and secluded campsites.

Cascade Lake has small boats for rent–no motors allowed–for quiet fishing or just plain loafing, and a swimming beach popular with youngsters. Picnic and camping areas with basic facilities for family use are located nearby and are so popular reservations are essential much of the year. For more advanced campers and anglers there are several other lakes at higher altitudes, all well stocked, and mile upon mile of unspoiled forest and mountain trails.

Stone lookout tower on Mount Constitution

But the chief attraction at Moran State Park is certainly the summit of Mount Constitution, from which one may enjoy as breath-taking a view of water, island, and mountain beauty as can be imagined. From the top of a stone lookout tower, exactly a half mile above the level of the sea, one looks out in all directions upon the island-studded, blue-green waters of Washington Sound –Eliza's "indescribable archipelago," all the more incredible for seeing it in one 360-degree panorama.

No artist could paint such a picture. No camera has ever properly recorded it. On a reasonably fair day the American mainland from Blaine to Mount Vernon, as well as the Canadian Gulf Islands and the cities of Vancouver and Victoria, are clearly seen. Mount Baker and, on really clear days, Mount Rainier are beautiful to behold.

The view is only bounded on the far north, west, and east by mountains, and on the south by the smog of civilization.

In former times, ascending Mount Constitution was only possible on foot, and the trip up and back constituted a full day's outing. Even so, islanders considered it as much spiritual as physical exercise, and many made it a kind of annual pilgrimage.

63

Back in 1912 the first car to make it to the top–a Model T Ford–was completely reduced to junk by the trip. Today there is a good road to the summit, part of it built by Robert Moran as a further gift to the state. Its two miles of fairly steep grades and switchbacks are not recommended for buses and trailers, but even bicyclists routinely make it to the top these days–though one wants to be in good condition for that!

After Mrs. Moran died in 1939, Moran sold Rosario to Donald Rheem, a part-owner of Paramount Pictures. (It was Rheem who added movie projection equipment to the music room.) Rheem and his wife lived a retiring life there for some years. Then in 1960 Gilbert Geiser, former mayor of Mountlake Terrace, acquired the property and began turning it into the premier all-year resort we know today. The mansion now serves as the main lodge, with an excellent dining room and cocktail lounge. Motel-type units have been added in separate buildings nearby, along with a boatel for visiting yachtsmen, a landing ramp for seaplanes and other facilities.

Apparently the Islands agreed with Robert Moran for he lived, not six months, but 39 years after coming to Orcas Island. Like so many others before and after him, he found the island's quiet beauty and calming peacefulness the kind of medicine you can't buy in drugstores. Robert Moran spent a million dollars or more on Orcas–in an era when a million was a very great deal of money indeed–but he always said it was the best bargain he ever struck.

Chapter Nine

Lopez and Shaw

*7*he first ferry stop out of Anacortes is at Upright Head, Lopez Island. Lopez is the third largest of the San Juans, is the third most populous island, and is as flat as the other islands are hilly. This makes it extremely popular with bicyclists, who descend on the island in greater numbers with each passing year.

The bikers' leisurely enjoyment of Lopez' quiet country roads and bucolic vistas pretty well symbolizes the slower pace of life here, and of change. Lopez is the last of the islands where vehicle traffic is infrequent enough that drivers still wave when meeting other cars, on the theory that if they don't know the other driver–they should.

But changes do occur, even on Lopez, even for instance in how people say the name of this island. Old-timers, who still pronounce Lopez to rhyme softly with "opus," wince at hearing the newer-comers' raspy "LOH-pezz," but know they're outnumbered.

Lopez is the one island where it is still possible to make a living–but just barely–by farming. Berries and other fruit, including grapes for wine-making, vegetables, grains, poultry and livestock are still raised on Lopez farms, though not nearly so much as in years gone by. Not that the soil and climate are any less favorable for agriculture than before, but soaring land values and the high costs of labor and shipping have taken most of the profit out of it.

In former times most Lopezians wrested their living from the land, or the sea. Turn-of-the-century orchards produced phenomenally, with tons of apples, cherries, prunes and strawberries being shipped to city markets and commanding excellent prices. Dairying was also profitable. The island had its own creamery and sent great quantities of butter and cream to Puget Sound markets along with eggs, poultry, and other products. In 1930 there were 134 farms on the island, which was also said to have the advantage that its tax rate was the lowest in the state.

The fishing industry, too, was in high gear during the early part of the century. Some of the catches recorded, even in ordinary years, seem unbelievable today. In an average season forty or fifty outfits, employing more than 400 men, filled the entire bay off the southern coast of Lopez with every conceivable type of craft and took a million to a million and a half fish from the sea. Most of the catch was taken to the mainland for canning.

A few companies tried salting and barreling the fish on Lopez, but most found this an unsatisfactory arrangement: the fish invariably came in faster than they could be barreled, which caused thousands of fish to be lost through spoilage.

Old-timers used to tell of salmon running so thick one could almost walk across San Juan Channel on their backs. Purse seiners occasionally found their nets so heavily loaded the catches could not be lifted into the boats. In 1901, half a million fish spoiled when the industry ran completely out of salt, barrels, and transportation.

Most of this activity centered around Mackaye Harbor, at the south end of Lopez, where the little village of Richardson became, in season, the busiest port in the San Juans. It was the first landing for many steamers coming from Seattle, and the wharf was always loaded with stacks of cordwood for the puffers' fires. The town was named for George Richardson, who settled there in 1871. The island's first post office was at Richardson, as was the island's earliest public hall–a combination church and social center. Three fish canneries, a warehouse, hotel, general store and blacksmith shop made Richardson a busy place in its day.

In 1916 a spectacular fire occurred at Richardson when sparks from a purse seine boat's exhaust ignited fuel leaked onto the water from an oil company supply ship. The 11-ton purse seiner, which had just arrived at the wharf, burst into flame, as did much of the bay's surface. One man scrambled to the dock in safety but three others, trapped below-deck, were obliged to swim for it through the burning oil and suffered horrible injuries. The purse seine boat was totally destroyed, as were the wharf, warehouse, fuel storage tanks and an adjacent cannery. The fire burned for hours. Fortunately the wind kept blowing off-shore all that time, or the rest of the village would no doubt have gone as well.

Among the spared buildings was the historic Richardson General Merchandise Store, which was established in May 1890 by

Robert Kindleyside and acquired, that year of the disastrous fire, by Ira Lundy. Lundy kept store there until his death in a car accident in 1931, after which his son and daughter-in-law took it over and ran it for another half-century and more.

The store itself changed little in all that time, but became something of a showplace as one of America's last old-time country emporiums. Not just Lopezians grieved when, in October 1990, fire started in a faulty appliance and burned the century-old store to the ground.

Richardson's decline began with the arrival of auto ferry service back in the 1920s. Steamer traffic to the island's southern end fell off sharply and the center of activity moved northward. The chief community on the island became the village of Lopez, located on Fisherman Bay on the island's west coast. Today the town has the island's only post office, as well as a church, inn, restaurant, grocery store and a number of other shops and businesses.

Old-timers used to say life on Lopez was so healthy, they had to kill a man to start a cemetery. The man that got killed was one John Anderson, a former shoemaker who lived and farmed on the eastern shores of Lopez at what is known as Sperry Point. Anderson had a "breachy" cow that wandered once too often onto the property of his neighbor, John Kay, with whom Anderson had never been too friendly. The two men got into a monumental fistfight which ended with Kay pulling a pistol and shooting Anderson dead.

Some on Lopez were all for stringing Kay up to the nearest tree, but cool heads prevailed and Kay was duly tried, convicted and sentenced to prison for his crime.

Sperry Point is Lopez Island's "big toe" protruding toward Lopez Pass opposite Decatur Island. In the summertime this 380-acre peninsula and the waters that all but surround it ring with the voices of youngsters happily attending idyllic Camp Nor-'Wester. A beloved and long-time institution in the San Juans, the camp was started in 1935 by Frank C. Henderson on property leased from the Roche Harbor Lime Company at Westcott Bay, San Juan Island. When the lime company declined to renew the lease after a few years, Henderson moved the operation to its present site on Lopez.

Frank and Lucille Henderson ran the camps–one for boys, one for girls–until their retirement in 1966, when it appeared the camps would have to close. Finally a private group of investors, many of them former Henderson campers, pooled resources and bought the property. Booth Gardner, future Washington State governor, headed the consortium. Besides swimming, hiking and such standard outdoor activities, the camp goes in strong for Indian lore, with expert counselors to make sure it is all done with as much authenticity as possible. Colorful "potlatch" celebrations are held in a 45-by-50 foot Indian house, a careful replica of the ceremonial houses built by the Kwakiutls of British Columbia. The Kwakiutl house, along with a 35-foot Haida-style Indian canoe, totem pole and other objects at the camp are largely the work of Northwest Indian art expert Bill Holm. Holm has been associated with the camp since 1940, when he was a teenage camper there.

Summertime fun at Camp Nor'Wester

There is a surprise in store for first-time visitors and ferry-riders when the boat leaves Lopez and, Orcas-bound, heads into its next landing at Shaw Island. On most occasions they will behold the dock being adroitly operated by Franciscan nuns, their sedate brown habits swinging gaily as these ladies go about their tasks of operating the transfer span and directing traffic. The nuns also run the adjacent Little Portion Store, the island's one and only commercial establishment. The store not only sells groceries, feed, seed, building supplies, hardware and gasoline, but has the island's only post office and is its principal gathering place and social center.

There are in fact three Catholic religious orders on Shaw, including the Order of the Benedictines which has a monastery on the island.

Shaw is located at the geometric center of the San Juan archipelago, and so is sometimes called "the Hub." The Wilkes expedition named it for John D. Shaw, who served prominently in the Algerian War of 1816. It is the "smallest of the biggest" islands in the group. Shaw was one of the last islands to get ferry service, back in 1930; and for years after that, the boats only stopped there on a flag signal.

Lime quarries, a fish cannery and a small shipbuilding operation once offered Shaw islanders employment. Today all that is gone, and the island is unique in having virtually no tourist-oriented facilities, either. There are a couple of smallish parks, though, and one of them—Indian Cove, on the southern coast—has a hard-packed sandy beach said to be the finest in the San Juans. Excellent (but limited) camping facilities are found in the park, which was once part of a military reserve, and subsequently purchased from the U.S. government with money donated by island residents.

Another goodly chunk of Shaw's real estate was, more recently, donated to the three Catholic groups by a large land-owner. Most of the rest belongs to private individuals who treasure their privacy and the slow pace of island life. Roads are mostly inland and afford visitors little access to, or even views of, the picturesque shoreline.

If you do tour Shaw, you'll want to pause at the island's major inland crossroad to see a little cluster of three attractive buildings. One is a rustic library, tastefully designed and constructed of cedar by local people. Next to it is a small museum, built of timbers from Shaw's first, log-cabin post office. The third structure, which is on the National Register of Historic Places, is Shaw's picturesque "little red schoolhouse." Not a restored curiosity, but one of America's last remaining and fully operating one-room schools, it evokes a gentler era–an era that has, sadly, long since ended almost everywhere but here.

Chapter Ten

Waldron—the Last Frontier

*T*here is no ferry landing at Waldron, nor is there likely to be one, as the island has no deep-water harbor. There is a good dock at Cowlitz Bay, on the southern shore, but this is both reef-bound and open to southeast and southwest storms, so that in rough weather even small boats have difficulty getting in. In the days when a scheduled mail and freight boat served the San Juans, when that boat's skipper encountered a severe blow he used to take her up into a more protected cove on President Channel, wrap the first-class mail in a slicker, and toss it to an islander in a rowboat.

But this is an old story to rock-bound, steep-rimmed Mail Bay, which got its name a century ago when Col. Enoch May used it as the "terminus" of his mail run, via leaky canoe, from West Beach on Orcas. The government paid May the munificent sum of approximately $30 a month to risk his life and the U.S. mail in treacherous President Channel twice a week. Once landed, May had to climb the nearly perpendicular cliffs surrounding Mail Bay to deliver his pouch to the island's postmaster, several miles inland. The path up the cliff can still be seen, but it is an ascent you don't want to tackle without tough knees and sharp fingernails.

In the years since then postal officials have tried various schemes to get mail to Waldron, contracting with boats of various sizes and even–for a time–flying it over in small planes, but in the end have come back to a variation on that century-old theme: shuttling it from Orcas' west shore in a small boat. Only this boat has a motor, and makes the Waldron trip THREE times a week.

Mail has always had a special significance on this island, in some ways the most remote of the populated San Juans. "Mail day" is the big social event on Waldron; it is a time when families from all over the island gather at the little log post office on Cowlitz Bay, not only to despatch and receive mail, but to do some neighborly visiting, catch up on the news, and exchange the inevitable island gossip.

71

Life seems to move more slowly on Waldron than almost anywhere else. Clocks are little esteemed. There is no public electricity, no telephone lines, no community water, and with few exceptions no inside plumbing. Waldronites are almost by definition people who prefer doing without these modern conveniences. Some are descendants of pioneer families who've always lived this way, but most are more recent arrivals, intent on recapturing a simpler but hardier way of life that's all but disappeared elsewhere.

There are a few beat-up old cars on the island but the narrow, unpaved roads are so overhung with brush and trees that the really ancient models' open door handles have been turned backward so as not to catch on them. Cars move so slowly that most drivers rarely shift above second gear. The only way you get a car onto Waldron to begin with is by landing it on the beach as freight, and once there, island cars stay 'til they wear out or rust out.

Waldron's population is growing, along with that of the other islands, but still numbers well under a hundred people. Some years ago there were a third as many. To keep their little rustic school going, residents had to advertise for a teacher–preferably one with children of her own to swell the number of scholars to the minimum required for state funding. Back in 1899, by contrast, there were 24 children in school and as many more due to start the next year. One Waldronite wrote the San Juan Islander: "If we could have as regular mail service as we have children, we would be satisifed."

That first Waldron schoolhouse–a picturesque one-room log cabin in the center of the island–was built in 1897 at a price of great bitterness to all, and financial hardship to many. Families with children voted for the school building, but in many cases these same families were not paying taxes, as they had not yet "proved up" their homestead claims; while those who were taxed were largely bachelors and families with no children. Taxes ran as high as $150 a year; most landowners had to go into debt to pay them, and a few lost their homes altogether.

One of the first teachers was Ethan Allen, Sr., usually called "Old Ethan" by Waldronites, and once known throughout the Islands as "the Sage of the San Juans." This kindly, white-haired, philosophical man, himself largely self-educated, was appointed Superintendant of Schools for San Juan County in 1898. In the years that followed, Allen rowed more than 10,000 miles in his home-made boat, keeping in touch with the county's 27 schools, and commuting to his "office" in Friday Harbor.

Waldron is a laid-back, peaceable kind of place today, but it was not always so. The island's very first settler, "Nowitka Jim" Cowan (*nowitka* meaning approximately "yeah, sure" in Chinook), was found murdered near his Cowlitz Bay shack back in 1868. The case was never solved, but a prime suspect was an Indian, Skookum Tom, who was wanted for one murder in British Columbia and suspected of another on Orcas. Tom camped out on Matia Island, perhaps because it is near the boundary line where he could retreat in either direction, should the law from one side or the other come after him.

Cowan's place passed to one J. T. Oldham. He in turn sold out to Sinclair McDonald, who became Waldron's postmaster in 1883. Charles Ludwig, in his excellent history of Waldron, tells of McDonald's involvement in an enterprise known as the "Lucy Bean Mission." It was during McDonald's tenure as postmaster that large packages of clothing began arriving at the Waldron post office, addressed to the "mission." There is a record of a William Bean living on Waldron at the time, but no Lucy. Some say McDonald himself was the "mission"–at least he managed to dispose of the articles in a manner that did not leave him any *poorer* than before.

After a while a committee, representing the Eastern churches which were contributing to the Lucy Bean enterprise, paid a surprise visit to Waldron and discovered that "Lucy's" letters describing the great work that was being done among the heathen natives had been–to say the least–exaggerated, and McDonald's missionary career quite suddenly ended. Not too long afterward his career as postmaster likewise came to a close.

Early settlers included Edouard Graignic and Louis LaPorte, French sailors who jumped ship in Victoria, married Indian wives, and before long had made their home on Waldron. The Graignic family went into the herring business: they fished by lighting beach fires at night, which attracted the fish to the shore, and then rowing around the fish with their nets.

Graignic periodically took their catch, neatly packed in hand-made wooden boxes, to Victoria in his sloop, the *City of Paris*.

The Graignics were a large family and a number of their descendants still live on Waldron and other islands of the San Juan group. A son, Peter, was the first white child to be born on Waldron, and is said to have been able to sail the family sloop to Victoria and back, alone, at the age of seven. Prosper, another son, is claimed to have been the Northwest's most prolific rum-runner in Prohibition days.

Aside from running rum and Indian missions, the leading industries on Waldron were fishing, farming, some logging, and stone quarrying. Waldron and one or two other islands have large quantities of excellent grades of sandstone, much used for paving city streets around the turn of the century. Several companies operated quarries there in that bygone time, including the Seattle Paving Co. and the Ellis Granite Co., who between them cobbled many a street in Seattle, Tacoma, and elsewhere. They also provided reasonably steady employment for 30 or 40 men on Waldron between 1903 and 1909.

A third company which ran a large operation for a year or two was Savage & Scofield, of Tacoma, who loaded stone on barges, converted from old windjammer sailing ships, and towed them by tug to the Columbia River, where the company was building the Grays Harbor jetty.

In 1908 the quarry workers formed a union, called the International Quarry Workers Union of Waldron Island, and led by a fiery Irishman, Mickey Boyle. About the same time the union handed the companies then operating on Waldron a list of wage demands, a $400,000 contract which one of the companies thought it had, fell through; a second was so far behind in paying wages the men had "attached" the company's stockpile of paving blocks as they were about to be shipped to Tacoma; and the third company, operating on a frayed shoestring anyway, decided it was time to fold up, too. Ludwig relates in his manuscript how the men, instead of getting a pay raise, guaranteed incomes, and so on, were deserted by Boyle, and came home from work one evening to find themselves with "no work, no union, no food, no nothing."

More recently Waldron has been home to a number of writers and artists. The first of these were June and Farrar Burn who homesteaded Sentinel Island–the last of the islands to be so claimed–and later settled on Waldron's Fishery Point, where the Graignics used to catch and smoke their herring. Farrar, whose brother Bob made the bazooka famous during radio's heyday, was a song-writer and one-time radio personality. June authored the popular book *Living High*, which describes the couple's early experiences in the San Juans and elsewhere. A daughter-in-law, Doe Burn, made her mark as an illustrator while residing on Waldron.

Norman McDonald, who spent part of his boyhood on Orcas Island–his father was a pioneer storekeeper at Olga–retired to Waldron to become, in his seventies, a successful novelist. His books include *Song of the Axe*, a rollicking fine story with the San Juans as a setting, and several others with Northwest backdrops.

In 1933 Jim and Frances Lovering arrived on Waldron to honeymoon, and to look over property Jim's brother, a New Yorker, had just purchased ("site unseen" as Frances put it) at the recommendation of his friends the Burns. The Depression was on, the newlyweds' net worth just then was something like two dollars, and while Jim was a licensed deep-sea mariner there was no berth in immediate prospect. As things turned out the brother never did spend much time on Waldron, but Jim and Frances quickly fell in love with the place and decided to stay. Over the years they raised and sold chickens, fished and farmed and dairied and milled lumber and kept a store, and periodically Jim would ship out on some freighter or other when a little extra capital needed raising.

Along with her other activities, Frances was for many years Waldron correspondent for the Friday Harbor Journal. Her weekly column, replete with its down-home wit and delightfully mangled syntax, was arguably the best thing in the paper. Readers who'd never set foot on Waldron in their lives turned to *The Waldron Word* first thing to chuckle over the latest doings of people they'd never met. Years later Frances wrote an engaging memoir of her life on Waldron, called *Island Ebb and Flow*. Her old columns, preserved as clippings stuffed in a shoebox, provided much of the material.

Communication with the outside world has traditionally been a serious matter on Waldron. In the past, the island had none, except as provided by the mail boat's not always dependable schedule. When the need was dire, a bedsheet spread between two poles on the beach would hopefully attract the attention of a passing boat or plane. With the advent of regular plane service, Waldronites could at least send messages off with the pilot; the answers, in many cases, were dropped from the next plane, tied to a rock, with a streamer attached to it.

When Citizens Band radios were first introduced back in the sixties, island people were among the first to make use of them. In spite of their limited range, and susceptibility to annoying interference, for lack of anything better they were a communications breakthrough. At least three homes on Waldron were among the first to become CB equipped, along with any number of other telephone-less residences and at least one general store in the Islands. Even the hitherto radio-less sheriff's department used CB's briefly, and on Orcas, the home of Roger and Huldah Purdue became for a time the county's unofficial message center, maintaining a 24-hour standby for emergency traffic, besides coordinating fire, police, and airplane despatching.

But as the CB bands quickly filled with the inane chatter of countless "good buddies" coast-to-coast, the little five-watt sets have become increasingly less useful. Beginning in the seventies however there have been steady improvements in other means of communications county-wide. Touch-tone phones, 911 emergency calls, sophisticated sheriff, fire and rescue car despatching, computer networking, fax machines and pagers and all the rest of the modern communications panoply are as commonplace here as elsewhere.

Cellular phones in particular mean that no island needs to be really remote from the outside world any longer. There are those on Waldron who shake their heads at the idea, but even there you can see people chatting casually into those cordless hand-held antenna-sprouting contraptions with all the buttons and flashing digits on them. To this extent at least, even this island seems to have finally entered the high-tech world of today.

Chapter Eleven

When Is an Island?

*T*here are, as has already been pointed out, well over 400 separate land masses–including rocks, reefs, islets and full-sized islands–in the San Juan archipelago. Each has its own character, and over the years, many have had "characters" living on them, too.

Today one is more apt to find on the smaller islands quite ordinary people, except that they have done something positive about the yearning to be island dwellers, instead of just dreaming about it. Often these "rugged individualists" are retired people who have been successful in business and are now equally successful at being leisurely.

But in the old days, before cell phones, radios and airplanes, and especially before gas-powered boats, island living was far rougher and lonelier. Anyone living on an island *alone* was considered the ultimate recluse.

When Captain Elvin Smith settled on Matia in 1892 the county paper had soon tacked on him the title, "the hermit of Matia Island." Smith, a robust six-footer, was a Civil War veteran who fought so bravely he was raised from the ranks to command a company. But after the war, so the story has it, his battlefield commission was disallowed on some technicality; and when in addition he suffered an unhappy love affair, he chucked it all and came west, to forget.

Smith squatted on Matia thinking the island would soon be opened for homesteading, but the government never did release Matia. Still Smith had fallen in love with the island and spent all the rest of his days there.

Smith got his staple supplies from Orcas once a week, rowing across to North Beach regularly every Saturday in his little skiff. Later he got one of the first outboard motor boats in the county.

Smith's solitary career ended in 1921 when he and a wartime companion perished in a storm while returning to Matia from visiting friends on Orcas. Smith was 86 then and still hale and

77

hearty, but–like so many others before and since–he and his old friend went to watery graves from which their bodies were never recovered.

Today Matia (or "Matey" as old-time islanders used to call it) is a federal bird refuge. Dozens of species from bitterns and sea parrots to black shags and humming birds can be seen at appropriate seasons. There is a small state park and campground on the northeast corner of the island, along with moorage for a few small boats, and several good inland trails, should you decide to come see for yourself the island Smith–and many others–have considered the most beautiful of all the San Juans.

Matia is long and narrow, like the top part of an exclamation mark, and is "dotted" so to speak by little Puffin Island, off the southeast end. There is no record of anyone ever living on Puffin, but in the very old days the Canadian Indians used to camp there in the spring to collect sea gull eggs and the sea lettuce which grows in abundant beds between the two islands.

Sucia Island, off to the northwest, is a 520-acre chunk of limestone, anciently scoured by retreating glaciers to form a fantastic conglomeration of cliffs, bays, rocks, inlets and islets. A one-time military preserve supposedly vital to our coastal defense, Sucia was later released for private ownership and ultimately bought up by Northwest yacht clubs and boating enthusiasts who presented it to the State as a marine park. Today it is the most popular park of its kind, and with good reason.

Back in 1902 a company was formed to quarry Sucia's abundant limestone, much of which wound up as street pavings in Seattle and other Puget Sound communities.

Captain and Mrs. William Harnden lived on Sucia for some twenty years after the quarry shut down, and raised a fine family of five girls there. Harnden also operated a popular excursion boat, the *Tulip King*. After their home burned down in the thirties, Harnden simply piled their surviving goods onto a salvaged scow, hauled it across to North Beach on Orcas, beached the scow and built a new house around it. He called the place "Harbor Lights."

The Harndens' children and grandchildren came to love Sucia and to know all its many coves and bays. Often they played in the two "smuggler's caves" reputed to have been used by rum-runners in Prohibition times. One of the caves, in Blind Bay, can be entered only at low tide. At high tide the entrance is completely hidden.

Farther northwest, Patos too was a way-point for smuggling gangs in the old days. Many exciting adventures that occurred there have been written down in a book by Helene Glidden, whose father was a lighthouse keeper at Patos' Alden Point light. Family members and other characters are given different names, but Mrs. Glidden assures us the events in *A Light on the Island* are all true.

Mrs. Glidden's mother was a relative of Theodore Roosevelt's. "Teddy" visited them once on a hush-hush fishing trip, and brought with him as presents for the children a pair of stuffed Australian koalas–the original teddy bears.

Patos by the way still has its all-important lighthouse but the days are gone when keepers and their families lived there in romantic isolation. There are no inhabitants, and the light operates remotely from a prosaic Coast Guard office down-Sound.

The northwesternmost of the San Juans are Stuart and Johns, so close they are virtually one island. About half a hundred people live here, and the only village is Prevost, a sort of last American outpost before one enters Canadian waters. Stuart has been home to many interesting people down through the years, but none, perhaps, more fascinating than the mysterious individual known as "Littlewolf," a reclusive individual who claimed to have been abandoned as a child and ultimately raised by wolves. He told wonderfully entertaining stories (some of which may even be true) about his long life as a fisherman, rum-runner, and all-around adventurer. As a sort of hobby, "Littlewolf" fashioned copper bracelets from used electric company wire, that were supposed to ward off arthritis. He gave them away free to anyone who visited his Stuart Island cabin and modestly claimed, before his death in 1986, to have made "about three million" of them.

Tragedy struck the Stuart community in 1961 when an 18-foot outboard-powered dory bearing James Hendron and his family, including six children, caught fire and burned somewhere between San Juan and Stuart Islands. There were no survivors and only one body, that of one-year-old Jeffrey, was recovered. The family were heading home from Roche Harbor the day after Christmas, and were not missed until after the holidays when nobody showed up for school–the Hendron children were the entire student body!

The late Bill Chevalier, who lived all his life in the San Juans, mostly working on the ferries and other vessels, recalled that there were 25 in the little school on Stuart when he was a boy. The Chevaliers actually lived on nearby Spieden. Bill would row across to school each day, picking up other kids along the Stuart shoreline as he went.

Bill's dad was Ed Chevalier who, with his new bride, moved to Spieden in 1894. They lived there for 45 years and Ed became known all around the county as the respected "King of Spieden Island."

Spieden is a quiet island, interesting because one side of it is as bald as, on the other side, the trees are thick. Experts use photographs of the island to demonstrate various theories about the action of prevailing winds in distributing vegetation.

In 1970 a Seattle taxidermy firm bought Spieden, renamed it "Safari Island," and stocked it with exotic (but technically domestic) wildlife, including rare varieties of deer, sheep, goats, game birds and other critters. The idea was to provide tired corporation executives with a way to hunt big game as a form of R and R–for a hefty fee, of course, and with the near certainty of bringing back as many trophies as one might care to pay for.

Island people joined with environmentalists, animal-rights devotees, state legislators, real hunters and people of ordinary good sense everywhere in opposing the project. Not many huntsmen responded to the company's slick brochures, but there were enough to spook the animals, many of whom swam across to San Juan and made colorful nuisances of themselves. The whole operation closed down after a couple of years. A great many of the animals stayed on Spieden, though, and provide a certain excitement to passing ferry-riders yet today.

Fifteen-acre Sentinel Island lies just off the tip of Spieden and adventurous ferryboat skippers sometimes pass through the narrow channel between them on the Sidney run. Sentinel is the island June and Farrar Burn homesteaded and called "Gumdrop Island," as mentioned a few pages back. As June described it, Sentinel was "like a park on top, with high grass, no underwood, no bracken, no salal, no Oregon grape–also no beach, no harbor, no water! Just the stems of trees (they are a good deal larger than stems today, though), high grass, deep moss and wild flowers. You can go to the top of Sentinel and leave the world behind."

Only you can't, any more. Sentinel is an eagle sanctuary now. It's owned by the Nature Conservancy, and visitors are not allowed.

Some of the prettiest scenery in the San Juans is in the island-studded passages between Shaw and Orcas' Steep Point. Here the water is broken with dozens of picturesque reefs and islets, many of them inhabited. On little Yellow Island–it's off the starboard side as the ferry heads north from Friday Harbor–Lew Dodd and his wife Tibby once built their dream house, low on the beach, using nothing but beachcombed materials. Even the furniture and most of the hardware was gleaned from the seas. Lew died there in 1960, in the fourth decade of what he called "the best life in the best county" he'd ever known.

Tibby stayed on alone for a number of years, with a little hand-held CB set as her only outside-world contact. There's a memorial to the Dodds on Yellow today, and although the island has been owned by the Nature Conservancy since 1980, visitors are permitted–but with restrictions.

Nearby are the Wasp Islands, said to be the haunt of pirates in bygone years, with many tales of supposed crimes–ranging from the emptying of fish traps to moonlight raids on neighboring gardens–attributed to them. Clare Tift on Shaw recalled finding on one of the islands a crude mold, carved out of wood, apparently for counterfeiting fifty-cent pieces.

Just over the channel is McConnell Island, where Dr. Thomas Thompson–a noted oceanographer and long-time director of the laboratories at Friday Harbor–lived with his family for many years. The island has the distinction of being the only one in the archipelago to sport a steam train, complete with a considerable distance of track. Built and maintained by the Thompsons, it was later removed to Anacortes where the train still makes a colorful appearance on special occasions.

The largest island in the area is Crane, just across narrow Pole Pass from Orcas. The 150-yard-wide passage is so named because Indians used to stretch nets across the water, supported by tall poles, to catch low-flying birds.

Blakeley's pioneer schoolhouse

There was a time when it took a great deal of adventurous spirit, but not a lot of cash to buy an island. Today it's the other way around, and taxes alone can cost you big. By contrast, one of the San Juans was actually *given away* some years ago, as first prize in a contest. It was a promotional stunt, of course, but it attracted lots of interest and bushels of entries from all over the country. For her essay on "Why I would like to live in the San Juan Islands" the winner—a Seattle woman, as chance would have it—was awarded little Deadman Island, off Lopez' Davis Point. The essay had to do with an island's being a good place to raise children, but apparently the writer never raised any children—or anything else—there, but rather traded the island in on a car.

Blakely Island, between the eastern half of Orcas and Lopez, is not a small island. It is privately owned and more or less off-limits to most visitors, however, so seems to fit the category of this chapter's look at the "lesser" San Juans. Blakely is known as the flying island of our archipelago. The nearest thing to a village on Blakely is a cluster of homes directly fronting on a hard-surfaced airstrip, which cuts across the island's southernmost point. As one would surmise, many of the residents use planes to commute to mainland jobs.

Most of the island is in as natural a state as when Paul Hubbs and a few others first explored it a century and more ago. Except for an abandoned schoolhouse a mile or so away, few traces remain now of the pioneer village of Thatcher, its once-busy sawmill or the gold mining venture that caused some turn-of-the-century excitement. The school however stands as a reminder of the county's most celebrated murder case.

It was a teacher at the school, Richard Straub, who was accused of brutally killing Leon Lanterman and wounding Lanterman's sister, Pauline Burns, in a potato field. (Potatoes loom large in our Islands' history.) Straub was apparently incensed at Mrs. Burns, a school board member, after he lost his teaching job.

Straub was apprehended and taken to Friday Harbor, where a mob formed and threatened to make their own "justice." Straub and a companion, who was later acquitted, were spirited out of the county's jail–a frame shed in back of the courthouse–into the woods for the night, and then taken to the mainland for safekeeping.

Straubwas tried, found guilty and sentenced to die on the gallows. Sheriff Newt Jones performed the execution–the only one ever in the San Juans–on April 23, 1897, inside a specially-built 16-foot board fence on the east side of the jail. Attendance was by invitation only, but rubberneckers were discovered watching from the upper floor of the Odd Fellows building (now the Whale Museum) across the street.

All of this so unnerved Sheriff Jones that he was reportedly never the same after the hanging. Straub's lawyer, after shouldering as much criticism from fellow townsmen as he could stand, left the county and is said to have taken his own life shortly thereafter.

Straub's body was buried in a small plot at Point Caution, near the marine station. The jailhouse, scene of the nearest thing to mob action the islands have known, moldered on–rarely used–until a few years ago when the state declared it unsafe and a disgrace, and ordered it torn down.

Chapter Twelve

Salt Chuck Country

*T*oday the waters of Washington Sound* are considered a barrier: something that separates the islands from each other and from the mainland, causing you to arrive early at a ferry dock, park your car in a sometimes maddeningly long line, and wait for one of the state's green and white "floating bridges" to haul you across. To our modern but land-bound automated culture, the San Juans might still be as remote as the Solomons, were it not for the ferries.

But for centuries it was the other way around. The great inland sea was the broad highway linking the Islands to the rest of the Northwest Coast. Coastal Indians–expert canoe makers and sailors, but clumsy land travelers–ranged the nearly 2,000 miles of shoreline at will, but seldom penetrated inland to any extent. Trading (and warring) freely among the tribes separated by hundreds of liquid miles led to the development of their common auxiliary language, the Chinook Jargon, a sort of aboriginal Esperanto. True, the Jargon was enriched to its full usefulness after the coming of the Whites, but its bare bones existed long before that.

When the first paleface did make his appearance, it was by water, not overland. And when he decided to stay awhile, he nearly always chose to settle near the water, partly because food abounded there, but mostly because it afforded the most practical kind of transportation.

Inevitably the Islands' history is concerned with the steamboats and sidewheelers, packet boats and ferries, the sea captains and the smugglers, that plied the waters around and between them over the years.

The Hudson's Bay Company's pioneer steamer *Beaver* ran as needed between Victoria and the San Juans, up to the time of the Pig War. In 1861 the American government chartered the trim

*Technically, Puget Sound comprises waters roughly south of the strait; the area to the north, including the San Juans, is Washington Sound.

100-footer *Diana* to cary mail, troops and what have you to San Juan Town, which became its home port. The *Diana's* captain, Tom Wright, made the trip every month or so, interspersing side voyages to other Sound ports and even to Alaska.

Regular boat service began in 1873. The tug *Rose* carried mail to the Islands every second week on its way from Port Townsend to Whatcom (Bellingham). Later the *Etta White*, and then the *Dispatch*, made weekly trips over the same route.

The schooner *General Harney*, which brought the first U.S. troops to San Juan, also made frequent but unscheduled runs through the Islands. This Bellingham-built 80-footer—the first sailing vessel built in the Puget Sound country—carried most of the first livestock to the Islands, and hauled lime and brick from the San Juans to Seattle for the territorial university.

Schedules gradually increased until, in the nineties, the San Juans were enjoying daily service. Boats carrying mail, produce, and passengers included the *Phantom, Rustler, Teaser, Discovery,* and the *J. B. Libby.* The *Libby* later burned when its cargo of lime from Roche Harbor caught fire.

About 1893 the *Lydia Thompson*, 102 feet long with a 22-foot beam, started thrice-weekly service from Seattle to Whatcom via the Islands. The *Thompson* was not the most comfortable boat that ever sailed, and was not missed when replaced by the elegant *Rosalie* with its staterooms, dining room and social hall in July, 1907. When the company pulled the *Rosalie* off the run a few months later and put the *Lydia Thompson* back, the hue and cry could be heard all the way to Seattle's Colman Dock.

The following spring Inland Navigation Co. announced it was returning the *Rosalie* to the San Juan route and solemnly promised the hated *Thompson* would "never again" see service there. Three weeks later the *Rosalie* broke a tail shaft and the *Lydia Thompson* was back again.

As the Islands' commerce boomed, Washington Sound became filled with ships of all descriptions and on all sorts of schedules. Several home-owned vessels enjoyed good business, including Andrew Newhall's *Buckeye* and the 85-foot *Islander*, both built at Stockade Bay on Orcas. A second and larger *Islander*, afterward renamed the *Mohawk*, was built at the Friday Harbor shipyard of

Albert Jensen and Sons–a pioneer firm still going strong.

Other boats worthy of mention included the *Evangel*, commanded by Capt. Herbert Beecher, son of the famous evangelist, Rev. Henry Ward Beecher; the Shaw-built *Edna*; and the *Yale, Anglo-Saxon, Alvarene, City of Anacortes* and *Yankee II*, all operated by Capt. Bill Kasch.

The Coast Guard later cracked down on a few of the smaller boats, some of which could not measure up to the safety standards.

The crackdown came largely as the result of the tragic sinking of the passenger steamer *Clallam* in the Strait. It was in January, 1904, that the ship, within a year of its launching in Tacoma, foundered in a southeast storm with the loss of 51 lives–including every woman and child on board. The official investigation of the sinking turned up conflicting and inconclusive evidence as to the cause of the disaster, but it did spotlight the laxness in observing safety rules that was common all over the Sound at the time.

Twelve of the *Clallam*'s passengers were from the San Juans, including Joseph Sweeney and Eugene Hicks from Friday Harbor; Mr. and Mrs. William LaPlante, their infant daughter Verna, and Mr. LaPlante's brother Peter, from Orcas; William King, from Orcas; and Mr. and Mrs. Thomas Sullens and their three small children. The Sullens family, originally from Deer Harbor, were going to Mount Sicker, British Columbia, where Sullens had a mining company.

Eight of the twelve perished in the disaster. William LaPlante and Sweeney, Sullens and King were saved.

LaPlante and Sullens saw their families wiped out when a lifeboat overturned. Mrs. Sullens held her two-year-old daughter out of the water as long as she could. Someone climbed down to the water's edge on a rope and was about to take the child from her hands when a wave snatched them both away, and they went down.

Hicks was also in the lifeboat when it overturned, and was hauled out, more dead than alive, but in spite of being partially revived by artificial respiration, he never recovered his strength and later went down with the ship. Sweeney was pulled from the water at the end of a rope which somehow became entangled around his neck. King escaped from the lifeboat and afterward was named in newspaper accounts as the hero of the hour for his part in saving a

The Islander, later renamed the Mohawk, a product of the pioneer San Juan Island shipbuilding family Albert Jensen and Sons.

number of his fellow passengers.

The *Clallam* went down, after a night filled with horrors, midway between San Juan and Smith Islands. Survivors were finally taken aboard tugboats which had, ironically, been close by the whole time–but hadn't spotted the distress flares sent up in those pre-radio days.

Steamboating in the San Juans declined in the teens. In 1922 Capt. Harry Crosby started the first ferry service through the Islands, opening an era that continues to this day. Crosby, who began his career as a newsboy selling hand-printed extras during the big Seattle fire, had been skipper of his own boat since he was 13, and by the twenties had owned seven or eight boats, including the not-too-popular *Lydia Thompson.*

For the Anacortes-San Juan-Victoria run, Crosby bought an old 97-foot kelp harvesting scow, the *Harvester King,* and chartered the *Gleaner,* a stern-wheeler, to run opposite her. The run proved a financial success during the summer, but was closed down for the winter. The next spring Crosby sold the *Harvester King* and replaced it with the newly converted *City of Angeles* chartered from Joshua Green's Puget Sound Navigation Co. He also bought the *Robert Bridges*, a venerable passenger vessel of Seattle's mosquito fleet, turned her into an auto ferry and renamed her the *Mount Vernon*.

In 1924 Crosby sold out to the Puget Sound Navigation Co. (later part of the famed Black Ball Line) which operated the route continuously until it was taken over by the State of Washington in 1951.

Originally the ferry stops were Anacortes, Orcas, Roche Harbor, and Sidney. In 1926 Lopez was added, and the next year Friday Harbor. In 1928 Roche Harbor was omitted, and Shaw was added to the route in 1930.

The ferry Rosario was a regular on the San Juan Islands run for many years.
Puget Sound Maritime Historical Society

Capt. Sam Barlow as the youthful master of the Rosalie.

The early ferries carried freight as well as passengers, and at each stop a tractor-drawn train of narrow, freight-laden flatcars was the first thing to disembark. At first there were no adjustable slips, and ferries pulled up at ordinary wharves where freight elevators were used to raise vehicles and foot-passengers from deck to dock. Automobiles were driven onto the elevator beds across a pair of narrow planks, called "transfer boards"; this was too much for many women–and some men–drivers, so crewmen often drove their cars on and off for them.

By the thirties passenger steamers from Seattle had stopped running to the Islands, but San Juan-bound travelers could take a comfortable overnight boat like the *Sol Duc* to Anacortes and change to the ferry there. There was a connecting schedule but sometimes the steamers were late for some reason, and the ferry would be half way to Lopez before the night boat was met, steaming up Rosario Strait. The two vessels would tie up together, put a gangplank across, and exchange passengers in mid-channel.

Ferryboating in the San Juans became an art unmatched, perhaps, in any other corner of the world. Men like Sam Barlow, Ed Draper, Paddy Berneson, John Oldow and a dozen others perfected the science of navigating through narrow, twisting channels that would make a conventional four-striper blanch.

When the visibility was nil, San Juan ferries were navigated "on the horn"–that is, by listening to the echo of the boat's whistle, noting the direction of the returning sound, and counting the time it took to come back. Today's skippers use radar, of course, but that is after all just an electronic refinement of the same principle.

In a real pea-souper, those earlier skippers relied on any number of tricks to help pinpoint their position. Familiar sounds like a dog barking or roosters crowing helped. Close to the dock, the aid of an islander, beating on an oil drum with a club, was sometimes needed to find the first pilings leading to the slip.

Sam Barlow used to wear a broad-brimmed, black felt hat when the fog rolled in; he claimed he could hear echoes better with it on than with the usual captain's hat. Half-Indian, Barlow's keen senses of smell and hearing helped make him the all-time dean of ferryboaters in the Islands. He could pick up the odor of kelp–a sure sign of shallow water–at amazing distances, and could read an echo or outguess a current with uncanny precision. Even today, for all their sophisticated equipment, ferries occasionally (not often!) demolish docks or graze lurking reefs. It's claimed Barlow, in his 47-year career, made some twenty thousand trips in local waters and never scratched a ship.

Ferryboating in the thirties wasn't just a job, but a full-time calling. The Depression was on and jobs were hard to find. Puget Sound Navigation paid boatmen $50 a month plus "room and board"–meaning you lived (and worked) aboard your vessel day in and day out. If you wanted a day off, you had to find someone to take your place and pay him from your own pocket. For the public, though, service was good then, with up to four trips a day through the Islands in the summer, three of which went on to Sidney, B.C. Of course the ferries were much smaller and carried only a fraction as many vehicles as today's 160-car superferries.

Boatmen's unions were eventually formed which won ferry workers steadily improving wages and conditions, leading in turn to frequent rises in ferry tolls. In 1948 when State regulators refused to approve another whopping increase, the company announced plans to suspend service altogether. Washington State Governor Mon Wallgren stepped in with an offer to buy the ferry service. Three years and much bitter controversy later, the State did just that–and promptly raised the fares yet again.

Constant increases in traffic to the San Juans over the years have meant the need here for ever bigger and faster boats. In 1972 two Jumbo Class ferries were constructed specifically for the San Juans run, the *Spokane* and the *Walla Walla*, each carrying over 200 cars and running at 18 knots. Shortly after they were placed in service, however, it appeared that these vessels were simply too powerful for the tortuous Island routes–their wakes were causing damage to fragile shorelines. The jumbos were moved down-Sound, and it seems the 160-car superferries such as the Kaleetan and Elwha represent the limit in speed and size that the Islands run can handle–for now.

Chapter Thirteen

The San Juans Today—And Tomorrow

T raditionally, living in the magic San Juan Islands has been, if not always easy, at least comparatively uncomplicated. Islanders have treasured a lifestyle that was unhurried, honest and neighborly, and largely unfettered by governmental oversight or decree.

County government used to consist of a handful of helpful folk rattling around in their little red brick courthouse at Friday Harbor. Three county commissioners got together over lunch every month or so, and decided such weighty issues as which island roads needed grading. Each island had a part-time deputy sheriff or two, but there was little for them to do, since real crime in the San Juans was almost unheard of.

There were three lawyers in the county, one of whom was my grandfather. I can attest that his income from legal work was meager. Cases tried in court were rare, and years might go by without even one jury trial being held.

For decades the county's population held fairly steady at around 3500 people or so, and the taxes they paid were about as low as taxes get.

Today all this has changed. San Juan County is the fastest growing county in the state, the per-capita value of taxable property here is twice that of the next most heavily taxed county, and county bureaucrats can hardly build new offices, wings and buildings fast enough to accommodate their own burgeoning numbers.

The explosion in growth began in the decade of the seventies, which saw the population all but double. Since then, except for a brief leveling during the eighties' recession, growth has continued at anywhere from 2.5 to as much as 6% annually. The current population of San Juan County is something like 12,500 year-round people. You can figure twice that many in summer, counting seasonal residents and visitors.

Not only the numbers but the kinds of people living in the San Juans are changing. Relatively few now are working fishermen, loggers, ranchers, as before. Most jobs today are in the low-end service sector–resort and restaurant workers, souvenir-shop salespeople and the like–and in such growth industries as real estate and construction work. There are also significant numbers of self-employed professionals (including artists, writers, and certain kinds of entrepreneurs) who can basically live and work wherever they like.

Perhaps the largest single class of newcomers are the retirees–though the percentage of over-65s in the Islands is still not as high as in other parts of the state. In fact, recent statistics suggest that the percentage of retired people here is declining.

What is not declining is concern for what all this growth is doing to our community, our lifestyle and our livelihoods. The debate as to the benefits versus the drawbacks of growth goes on endlessly, and grows steadily more strident as the stakes rise ever higher.

There is no doubt that growth creates jobs and injects new money into the economy, but more than one study suggests that the heightened costs for services (new schools, more police presence, wider roads) more than sops up the increase, for a net loss to the community. There is also concern that today's population is less stable than it used to be. It is no longer true that you know everybody you run across in the store or on the street. Not all the newcomers behave as neighborly and civilly as one would like (though most do), and a few have brought along with them from the mainland the very problems of crime, drugs and abuse that others came here hoping to escape.

But it is the effect of growth on our environment that is the chief worry, and the chief source of conflict. For while part of the cherished tradition of the San Juans has been the freedom to do as one pleases, when one pleases with one's land, there are only so many trees to cut, so many wells to drill, so much wetland to drain and dry land to pave over, so many docks to build and shorelines to reshape before the character of the whole will be spoiled for us all.

With this in mind the county adopted, after several false starts, a Comprehensive Plan in 1979 that essentially prohibited the dividing of most land into parcels smaller than five acres. Together with other state and county regulations that have come into play, the Plan obliges landowners and developers to obtain permits before virtually any construction, land transaction, or change to the landscape can take place. Predictably, environmentalist groups feel the regulations are too permissive, while developers, builders and many landowners complain that the restrictions go too far.

The biggest complaint is that in trying to make the Plan flexible, its writers gave too much discretionary (some would say arbitrary) power to professionals hired by the county to enforce the Plan. This has led to a series of expensive and divisive lawsuits against the county, not to mention escalating costs for the seemingly endless process of studies, reports, permit applications, hearings and appeals required before any really significant development can take place.

More recently the county purposed to rewrite the Plan, and its accompanying regulations, nearer to the heart's desire of the Islands' citizenry. To this end hearings were held on each island and working groups were set up, composed of citizens representing all interests in the county, to try and come up with a consensus as to the amount and kind of regulations to be imposed, including just what results said regulations should be designed to achieve. The process has been going on for several years now, well behind schedule, and what seems to have emerged is that there is no such consensus. Like the cake that you can either have or eat, the dilemma remains the same: stifle growth and hurt people, or encourage it and hurt the islands.

Conventional wisdom down through the years held that overpopulation and overdevelopment of the San Juans could not take place for two reasons: limited transportation and limited water. As is often the case, conventional wisdom is turning out to be wrong.

For all the complaints of long waiting lines and faulty schedules, Washington State Ferries is clearly committed to providing–more or less–whatever service level is truly needed. More boats are to be built, and if all else fails, someone in Olympia will no doubt dust off an old plan to build bridges to and between the Islands. There will be howls of course, but the pressure to enable more and more people to get from here to there will be formidable.

As to fresh water in the Islands, the supply is certainly finite, as several years of lower than usual rainfall have demonstrated. New wells are being drilled all the time, with the result that old wells produce less and less, so that more and deeper ones have to be drilled to provide for the needs of the ever increasing numbers of households. The risk of salt water intruding into the deepest wells is very real. Not a few of the others go totally dry in summer, so that water-hauling is now a growing business.

In 1994, despite rigorous conservation measures, the entire town of Friday Harbor came within just days of totally exhausting its supply of fresh water. The town was poised to start barging in mainland water when the rains finally returned.

Today, more and more people are talking about desalination plants as the long-term solution to the county's water woes. A few such plants–small ones for private use–are already in operation, and questions about their environmental impact are adding to the county planners' concerns.

Recently there has been talk about possibly capping growth at, say, a manageable 2% a year. This could probably be done, for example by limiting the number of construction permits issued annually. It hardly seems likely, though, that the county would adopt such a draconian measure, and jeopardize the livelihoods of so many of its citizens. In any case, artificial limitations of that sort will simply drive up costs, hastening the day–every islander's nightmare–when the Islands become a playground for the rich.

Short of repealing the law of supply and demand, growth in the San Juans is going to continue. The Islands' appeal is as potent today as ever, and as people come and see and fall in love with what has more than once been called "paradise on earth," how can we fault them for succumbing to the magic–as each of us in our turn has done before?

With good will and sensitive management, problems will be solved, growth accommodated, the environment secured. We will see changes–but they will be changes in how we use and relate to this blessed bit of God's earth.

The Islands themselves, we have to believe, will surely endure, casting their spell as they always have, long after we are gone.

KLOSHE KAHKWA!

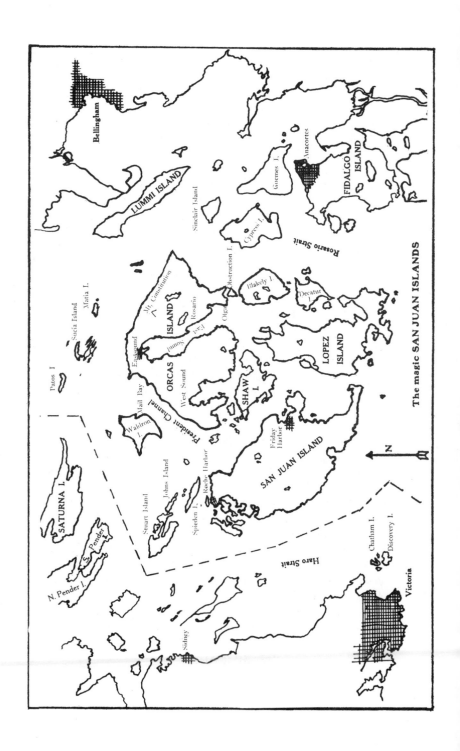

The magic SAN JUAN ISLANDS